D0923824

Better Golf from New Research

Better Golf from New Research

BY FRANK D. WERNER
AND RICHARD C. GREIG

Copyright © 2001 by Frank D. Werner

Published by Origin Inc, 3975 So. Hwy. 89, Jackson, WY 83001

Distributed by Tech Line Corp, 3975 So. Hwy. 89, Jackson, WY 83001

First Edition

Book design by Julie McIntyre

Printed in the United States of America

Publisher's Cataloging-in-Publication Data
(Provided by Quality Books, Inc.)

Werner, Frank D.
    Better golf from new research / Frank D. Werner,
  Richard C. Greig. -- 1st ed.
    p. cm.
    Includes bibliographical references and index.
    LCCN: 2001130536
    ISBN: 0-9677625-1-0

    1. Golf. I. Greig, Richard C. II. Title.

GV965.W47 2001   796.352
                QBI01-200747

WARNING/DISCLAIMER

The information and material contained in this book are provided as is, without warranty of any kind, express or implied, including without limitation any warranty concerning the accuracy, adequacy or completeness of such information and material or the results to be obtained from using such information or material. In no event shall the publisher or authors be liable for direct, indirect, incidental, or consequential damages arising out of the use of such information or material.

You must independently confirm or revise information or material from this book if used by you in cases where liability of any kind may be involved.

If you do not wish to be bound by the above, you may return the book to the distributor for a refund.

Table of Contents

Preface

Most of the material in this book is condensed from our earlier book, *How Golf Clubs Really Work and How to Optimize Their Designs*. That book was rather technically oriented and provided a technical record of our research. Most of the general text of that book is readable by the serious golfer. It has Technical Notes to separate many parts that were directed to the more technical golfer and to researchers and designers in the field. It provides the technical support for conclusions given here and gives much information which is new in golf. In the long term, we believe it will be a useful source book. Some readers may wish to refer to it for more detail in some areas, so we often refer to it as the *First Book* and its identity follows the Appendix.

How This Book Can Help Your Game

This book provides new information that is based on our experiments on golf and golfers and on analysis that has never been done before. Some of the content represents a significant departure from the conventional understanding. The Table of Contents indicates various helpful areas. Our research is explained in our first book, *How Golf Clubs Really Work and How to Optimize Their Designs* ©2000, hereafter referred to as the **First Book**. We undertook that work to improve club design. As you will see, some of this new research-based information can reduce your golf scores.

Perhaps the most important part of effective golf is a *repeatable* swing. A *good* swing is also highly desirable. However, this book offers no guidance on your swing. You will need a competent golf teacher and lots of practice for that. Here, you will find new ways to play better golf with the swing you already have, whether it is good or bad. This book also provides a wealth of information on the nature of golf shots and provides golfers with a keener understanding of the golfing environment (wind, turf conditions, etc.), but with no attempt to cover all aspects of golf.

Undoubtedly, some experienced golfers will not agree with all of our conclusions. In many cases, it is extremely difficult for them to be sure their conclusions are correct, based on their golfing experience. The reason is that there are dozens of variables (factors) involved in the game of golf that can dramatically affect results. These factors fall into categories such as:

- *Golfer psychology (whether the golfer feels optimistic, tired, or ill, etc.)*
- *Numerous club design factors which may or may not be well-suited to the golfer*
- *Environment (wind, weather conditions, temperature, etc.)*

In nearly all golfing situations, the effects caused by one factor will be different (often very different) if the values of other factors are changed. In more technical language, the effects of almost all of the variables interact with each other as opposed to having independent effects.

This interaction of interrelated factors often makes it nearly impossible to know from experience whether focusing on one particular factor alone can produce better or worse results. Furthermore, how do you know if one or more factors have important effects or negligible effects when all of the other factors are present? Even if you know all of the relevant design factors, how would you know which particular factors cause perceptible changes in the result and which combination of factors will produce the best results? A very common and misleading error in advertising and marketing has been to focus on a single helpful design factor (or any other factor) that has negligible effects when all factors are included in the combined result.

We believe that remarkable advances in understanding golfing performance have resulted over the decades from the deductions of practical experience and careful observation, in view of these difficulties.

Appropriate mathematical analysis (our computer model) of the interacting factors shows the effects of these numerous factors in the combined result and eliminates this problem, except for the psychological factors. A principal goal of our research has been to understand the individual factors and their effects, individually and in any combination. Most of these results are directly useful to golfers.

This book describes new and useful game-improvement information in useful, relatively non-technical, and golfer-friendly form, as compared with the more technical *First Book*. Where it was necessary to introduce some special terms, we have highlighted them in each chapter in **bold italics** where they first appear. Furthermore, we have included an appendix that lists and defines these new terms for easy reference. The complete citation for the *First Book* follows the Appendix.

Our research findings apply primarily to the driver, and are contained in the first 10 chapters. Many of these findings also apply to the other woods and irons. The 11th chapter is specifically devoted to putters.

As is common in golf books, we discuss all topics from the viewpoint of right-handed golfers. Left-handed golfers should simply reverse things as appropriate.

Chapter 1 (this chapter) outlines how you can improve your golf game by giving some of your time and attention to reading this book.

Chapter 2 describes a new aiming procedure that we think will be valuable to all levels of golfers. It should increase accuracy of full swings with all clubs. If you have slice or hook problems, this procedure is an almost instant cure when used properly. It will also be valuable if you wish to learn more about controlled slices and hooks.

Other chapters are concerned with:

- *Habitual golfer errors*

- *The effects of wind and better ways to estimate wind speed*

- *Judging how "tight" your lies may be and what you can do about it*

- *The effects of playing your ball back or forward in your stance*

You will also find helpful information about:

- *How to choose a driver or putter*
- *How to better understand club design features that enlarge the sweet spot*
- *How to choose club designs that reduce the scatter in direction and in distance of your shots*
- *How to choose the best combination of design factors that will produce your golf shot's maximum distance*

There were 2 principal goals in our research: (1) to minimize the degree of scatter for all golf shots and (2) for drivers and first fairway wood only, to achieve the maximum **CHD** (center hit distance). With irons, the maximum CHD does not apply since loft of the club chosen is what controls distance for your particular swing. Our research on CHD is continuing.

Most of what we discuss came from our extensive computer modeling of the ball-club impact, the flight of the ball, and the bounce and roll distance. In addition, we conducted numerous kinds of field-based tests on actual golfers. Most of our modeling predictions have been confirmed by the results of actual golfing experience, the ultimate test.

This technical work allowed us to discover the *optimum combination of club design features*. We are confident this will prove to be a significant contribution to the game of golf. This work also allowed us to determine what are the most important and least important errors made by golfers. For an example of our computer modeling system results, see Table 1-1.

We hope you will find that this book helps you to better understand what is going on when you play golf and what you can do about it to improve—and enjoy—your own game.

TABLE 1-1 *Effects of wind, weather, and altitude on flight of the ball. The first line is a reference for all of the others. This is for a well-designed driver, used by a golfer whose good center hits go 209 yards.* **B&R** *means "bounce and roll" distance (sometimes called* **ZBR**).

environmental conditions					hitting the fairway				trajectory			stop point		
wind speed mph	wind direction	altitude feet	temperature deg F	relative humidity %	velocity mph	spin rate rpm	azimuth deg	elevation deg	maximum height yds	flight distance yds	B&R distance yds	distance to left yds	forward distance yds	radial distance yds
0	**-**	**0**	**70**	**20**	**57.3**	**2215**	**-.4**	**-26.9**	**14.6**	**172.6**	**36.5**	**0**	**209.2**	**209.2**
0	-	**2000**	70	20	59.9	2230	-.3	-25.1	13.9	173.5	39.8	1	213.2	213.2
0	-	**6000**	70	20	65.4	2262	-.2	-21.9	12.6	173.8	46.4	-.4	220.2	220.2
0	-	0	**50**	20	56.2	2209	-.4	-27.8	14.9	172.0	35.2	-.1	207.2	207.2
0	-	0	**100**	20	59.1	2225	-.3	-25.7	14.1	173.3	38.7	.1	212.0	212.0
0	-	0	70	**10**	57.3	2215	-.4	-26.9	14.6	172.5	36.5	0	209.1	209.1
0	-	0	70	**90**	57.6	2217	-.4	-26.7	14.5	172.7	36.9	0	209.6	209.6
10	**Head**	0	70	20	47.3	2163	-.7	-36.3	16.9	166.0	23.7	-.3	189.7	189.7
30	**Head**	0	70	20	34.2	2053	-4.5	-75.3	22.9	129.8	-4.1	-.5	125.7	125.7
10	**Tail**	0	70	20	62.4	2265	-.2	-21.1	27.7	173.5	48.6	.3	222.1	222.1
30	**Tail**	0	70	20	85.4	2355	0	-15.0	9.9	164.3	69.5	.8	233.9	233.9
10	**From left**	0	70	20	58.0	2216	-8.6	-26.5	14.5	172.8	37.3	-15.6	209.4	210.0
30	**From left**	0	70	20	62.4	2234	-22.5	-23.8	13.8	171.6	42.6	-44.8	208.6	213.4

Aiming, Avoiding Slices, and Working the Ball

This chapter explains a new way to aim which we call FF Aiming because you look at the club face in 2 separate steps, as you will see. It allows you to easily avoid slices and to make controlled hooks or slices at will, without changing your swing. It can significantly improve the accuracy of your shots and lower your score. Balls, shafts, and clubheads have changed greatly over the years; we think the aiming process may be next.

Learning the FF Aiming Process

FF Aiming is our abbreviation for the "Face-Face" aiming process. We use this name to emphasize that the club face orientation should be adjusted twice: first, when you are gripping the club, and second, when you assume your stance. There are some important differences from conventional aiming, and much which is essentially unchanged. This discussion applies for all golf shots except for chip shots and putts, which have their own unique features. FF Aiming can help you get the best results with the swing you have. If your swing needs improvement, we can't help, but we urge you to see a golf instructor.

With FF aiming, you always use your normal, most comfortable grip and swing. The result is better accuracy (more shots on the fairway) as compared to conventional aiming, and for sound, fundamental physical reasons discussed below.

Study and practice Steps 1 and 2 below, to learn FF Aiming. These steps will show you the two club face adjustments to use when you first grip the club and then when you take your stance. Step 1 is for learning to get straight, un-curved shots and Step 2 is for learning to get the direction you want.

The FF Aiming process cures unwanted slices or hooks. It also gives guidance in "working the ball" so that you can generate controlled slices and hooks at will, as discussed later. You needn't worry about the specific design details of your club, such as an open or closed face angle, shaft offset, and whether you sole the club at the outset. Results are the same. Here is what you will learn:

- *The **regrip** step that controls **curvature** of the shot.*

- *The **turntable** step that controls **direction** of the shot.*

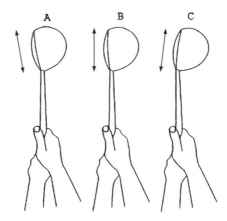

FIG. 2-1 *Examples of adjustment of the club face orientation to control or eliminate slices and hooks. Notice that the orientation of the hands does not change, whereas the club face does change. In this process, the grip is released, the club face orientation is readjusted, and then the same grip is assumed again. For example, if B represents your normal view of the club face, orienting the club face from B to A reduces slices, and hooks are reduced by orienting from B to C. Don't bother to aim the club face at the target in this adjustment.*

These are your basic means for producing straight shots which land where you want them to.

STEP 1: REGRIP. To *"regrip"* means to change the *club face* orientation and take a new grip *without* changing the orientation of your hands.

For the regrip step, you are only concerned with *curvature* of the shots, and not with direction of the shots. Study Figure 1 and its caption. On a practice tee when there is little wind, choose a club such as the driver and experiment to find the best club face orientation relative to your hands. For example, if you tend to slice, adjust the club face to be more closed as shown in A in the figure, take a new grip *without changing the orientation of your hands*, and make several hits. Experiment with the face more closed or less closed (regrip after each change) until you find the club face orientation which gives mostly straight, un-curved shots. If you tend to hook, experiment with a more open face orientation, as shown at C, instead of a closed face. *Consider only curvature of the shot and pay no attention to the target direction when you regrip and when you observe the results of these practice shots. Step 2 is where target direction is considered.*

Remember this regrip adjustment and use it when you are playing with this club. Also, remember always to use your normal stance and swing, and remember not to vary your grip orientation (such as a "strong" or "weak" grip). *Vary only the club face orientation and ignore the target direction.*

STEP 2: TURNTABLE. To *"turntable"* means to change the *club face* orientation by using the turntable movement described below.

For the turntable step, you are only concerned with direction of the shots, and not with curvature of the shots. Use the result already achieved from the regrip step and maintain your normal stance, then simply adjust the orientation of your stance as you hit shots by observing where the club face points relative to the target. When your shots are mostly going in the target direction, your stance is in the correct orientation. This adjustment in stance must be done with what we call the "turntable" rotation (like a lazy

Susan or a merry-go-round) where you keep the same stance posture but change the orientation of your stance. It is as if you were on a turntable with the ball at the center. You must learn to judge this turntable maneuver by observing where the club face points relative to the target. Changing the orientation of your stance is how this is accomplished. Don't merely move one foot or change your body position, posture, or your swing. *You must move both feet.* You may find that the best club face orientation points somewhat to the right or left of the target. *Be sure to take your normal swing in the new direction that corresponds to the new turntable orientation of your stance.* In other words, always use your normal swing relative to your stance. It may help to think of swinging toward an imaginary target that corresponds to the new turntable direction.

Remember the turntable club face orientation and use it when you are using this club. Also, remember to judge the turntable orientation by where the club face points and to adjust it by repositioning your feet to adjust the orientation of your stance.

Now you are producing shots with your driver which mostly fly straight (Step 1) and mostly go in the target direction (Step 2). You have learned the 2 essential club face orientations by looking at the club face while making the 2 different adjustments. You never need to learn to swing properly with a different grip or stance because you always use your normal grip and stance. With other clubs, you will probably find that somewhat different club face orientations are best, so you must also practice these two club face orientations with the other clubs, as is necessary with any aiming procedure.

It is important to realize that compared to short hitters, strong hitters will need relatively small changes of club face orientation to change the curvature of their shots. Very short hitters can't get much curvature of shots regardless of how they orient the club face.

Controlled Slices or Hooks

This subject is often called working the ball. To learn a slice, use a practice range. Redo Step 1 until the shots curve to the right as much as you want. When you get this orientation, maintain it and then redo Step 2 until the ball lands where you want it to land. Do the opposite to generate a hook. Notice that this is basically the same as learning to hit straight shots as described in Steps 1 and 2, except you are learning to get controlled, curved shots instead of straight shots. Practice is essential until you learn the new club face orientations in the above 2 steps that will produce the effect you want.

A Helpful Way to Judge the Club-Face-Hand Orientation

The shaft axis is a useful intermediate reference for orienting the club face and also for making sure the orientation of your hands is always the same. You do this by viewing the upper part of the club shaft axis relative to your hands and then viewing the lower part of the shaft axis relative to the club face. This replaces the process of looking from the hands to the club face. It is probably a little more accurate and is further discussed in Figure 2-2.

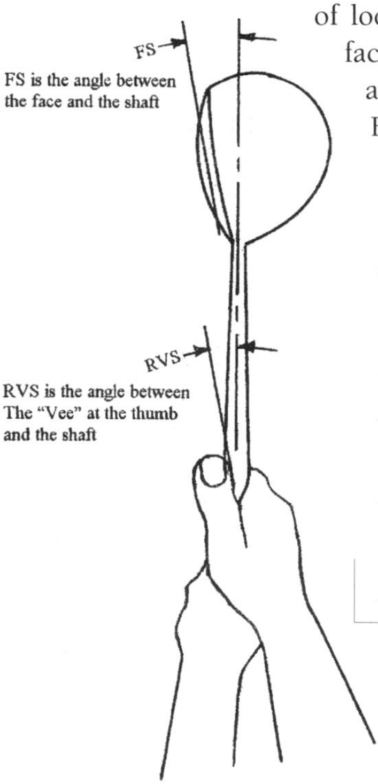

FS is the angle between the face and the shaft

RVS is the angle between The "Vee" at the thumb and the shaft

FIG. 2-2 *What to look at for the regrip step. The picture represents your view of a wood. FS in the drawing is the angle to adjust to in order to get straight shots and to control hooks and slices. Disregard the target direction when you adjust FS. RVS should always be what you use as your normal grip and should never change. The regrip step is an improvement over the conventional "strong" and "weak" grip procedure.*

Useful Suggestions

As you are playing a round, you may develop a slice or hook tendency or a left-right tendency may creep in. In this case, make small adjustments as needed in the regrip and/or turntable orientations.

If you use a tee with an iron for par 3 holes, the best club face orientations may be slightly different than for the same club on the fairway.

You may have the habit of soling your club at the beginning of your aiming routine. This generally doesn't give the correct face orientation that is needed for FF Aiming. Soling the club is not part of the process, but it is OK to start there, provided that you then do Steps 1 and 2 as described. You should also be aware that designed-in face angle or designed-in offset of a club has no effect. FF Aiming is independent of such matters and uses different and better ways to establish optimum club face orientation.

A side wind will curve your shots as you probably know, so don't do the learning process of FF Aiming when there is significant side wind. Some players may want to learn to counter the effects of side wind by learning the appropriate changes in aiming.

What to Look at on the Clubhead

When judging club face orientation with woods, it is important to look at the face, and you should ignore other features of the clubhead. Some players may prefer to look specifically at the toe and heel ends of the club face, while others may prefer to look at the bottom edge. In any case, it is the club face that you look at. With irons, it is best to look at the bottom edge of the club face.

Figure 2-3 shows changes in the club face orientation for small errors in the turntable step. They cause rather large lateral errors of the stop-point of a shot. Similar errors in the regrip step cause even larger errors. Careful observation of the club face orientation is very important.

FIG. 2-3 *If the center club face is the golfer's view of correct orientation in the turntable step, then the left club face is 2 degrees closed and the right one is 2 degrees open. These small changes are hard to see but cause lateral errors of 7 yards on a 200-yard drive and 10 yards on a 300-yard drive. Great care is needed when aiming.*

A Surprising Accuracy Benefit of FF Aiming

If you have hit a perfect shot except for an error in the regrip step, the ball will stop to one side or the other from where you want. That is to say, there is a lateral error. Computer analysis shows that if Step 2 is done correctly, the result is to reduce the lateral error caused by the regrip error. It turns out that for short drives, this means that only about 1/4th remains of the lateral error caused by the regrip error. For long drives, about 3/4th may remain, and even more for very long drives. *It pays to be very careful when choosing the club face orientation, especially at the turntable step.*

Summary of Benefits of FF Aiming

Here are 5 reasons why FF Aiming gives better accuracy of shots and lower golf scores:

1. **The turntable adjustment tends to reduce any error in the regrip step.** The error-reduction effect described in the preceding section is very important.

2. **There is no need to learn a strong or weak grip.** FF Aiming never requires that you learn to make a good swing after a sometimes-substantial change of grip from normal to weak or to strong. Such a change makes many golfers feel that their swing seems different.

3. **There is no need to learn an inside-out or outside-in swing.** When golfers try to change from their normal, comfortable swing, many are likely to feel uncomfortable with the change and find it difficult to make the new swing consistently. In FF aiming, you always use your normal, comfortable swing. We believe that you can groove your normal swing and repeat it more precisely than when you vary the swing from time to time.

4. **With FF Aiming, you specifically look at the club face rather than other features of the clubhead.** This is important. Most advice about aiming gives little or no detail about exactly what to look at on the clubhead.

5. **Improved confidence with drivers usually adds confidence for other shots.** We have often had interesting reports from golfers who say that when they are driving well, their confidence improves for their other shots, too. Presumably, psychologists are well aware of such effects.

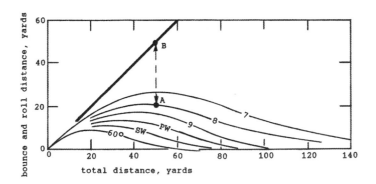

FIG. 3-1 *Bounce and roll distance for various clubs on level greens with Stimp 10. Flight distance (carry) is the total distance minus the bounce and roll distance. It is also shown in the example as the distance from point A to point B.*

The Basic Nature of Golf Shots

This chapter gives useful details for good, error-free golf shots for all clubs. You will find the height, flight distance, and bounce and roll distance with the shorter irons for full shots and for partial swings and chip shots. For all clubs, this chapter shows how golf shots are altered when the ball position is forward or rearward from the normal position.

Height, Flight, and Bounce and Roll Distances of Shots

Golfers have a general idea about how far their shots will fly and how far they will bounce and roll. Expert golfers may need little advice on this subject, but the details will be useful to most others. We abbreviate the bounce and roll distance as **B&R** distance. Once we developed our computer model, it provided such details, as shown here.

Figure 3-1 shows the bounce and roll distances for shots to average, level greens. Results are different with the various conditions of greens, so you should use this primarily as a basis for comparing various irons. B&R for longer irons and drivers cannot be presented in such compact form as in Figure 3-1.

The flight distance (carry) can also be found from the curves of Figure 3-1. For example, consider an 8-iron with 50-yard total distance. Find 50 on the horizontal scale and go up to the 8-iron curve at point A. From there, go left to find that bounce and roll is about 20 yards. The rest of the 50-yard total distance is flight, so it is 50 minus 20 which is 30 yards. This is also represented on the graph: to see this for this example, go from point A on up to the heavy straight line at point B to see the flight distance. This allows a quick visual comparison between the flight and the B&R distances for all shots from the short irons.

For short distances (less than about 5 yards), Figure 3-1 shows that most of the distance is bounce and roll for all clubs, and flight distance is very short. On the other hand, most of the distance is flight distance for the long shots as you would expect.

Greens usually slope toward the fairway and thus have shorter bounce and roll distances than shown and more shots backing up. For the longer shots, soft, wet soil on the green is also a large factor to decrease bounce and roll. Hard, dry greens can increase it to a sometimes troublesome extent. The Stimp reading alone doesn't tell the full story for long shots to the green. (**Stimp reading** measures whether the green is fast or slow.) Soft or hard greens cause large effects. Hardness of the green matters less for short shots which land at low speed and which make no ball marks on the green. In this case, Stimp and slope of the green are the main factors you need to consider.

Usually, you would not be concerned with trajectory height for partial swings, but sometimes there is a bush or tree which you must clear, or tree branches which your shot must go under. Our calculations show some simple approximations to guide you: *Maximum height for a 6 or 7-iron is about 17% of the expected flight distance for shots shorter than about 40 yards and increases to 50% or 60% for full shots. For pitching wedges and sand wedges with shots shorter that 40 yards, height is greater, up to about 25% of flight distance. Maximum height is reached at about half the expected flight distance for the shorter irons and for partial swings.*

Shots from drivers, from the longer irons, and shots which do not land on the green behave rather differently and can't be shown is a simple set of graphs like Figure 3-1. You will find more information in the *First Book*.

Fore-Aft Position of the Ball for Drivers

For driving, using a tall tee and playing the ball forward, even as much as 5 or 10 inches, can add several yards to your Center Hit Distance **(CHD)** in many cases. The gain in CHD is reduced or even reversed if your driver has too much loft. However, the gain will be impressive if you happen to have a driver with somewhat lower loft angle than what is best for your normal drives.

This advice about forward ball positioning applies only to drivers. It should also be noted that this positioning causes the ball to fly somewhat to the left, so some relearning is necessary in your aiming process. This is probably one reason why it is seldom done by golfers. Try positioning the ball forward at the driving range to see if you like it.

If you do, it is important to use a tall tee, even taller than the normally available tall tee, which is 2 3/4 inches. Unusual tees are sometimes available up to 4 1/2 inches or so. The additional distance is greater for short hitters than for long hitters. Chapter 8 of the *First Book* shows more detail.

As suggested above, playing the ball a few inches forward or rearward tends to make the ball go left or right, respectively. You must learn to adjust your aim direction by practice with such shots. The complications are worthwhile mainly for those who are seriously interested. Much practice and close observation of distance are necessary to evaluate the effects.

Increased distance for all other clubs requires playing the ball back rather than forward. This is because the main effect for shorter clubs from playing the ball back is to decrease their effective loft angles. You will find more about this in the next section.

Fore-Aft Position of the Ball for Clubs Shorter Than the 6-Iron

In deep grass or other special conditions, you may prefer to position the ball farther back than normal. Doing so increases shot distance and reduces height of the trajectory. The resulting shot distance depends mainly on head speed, loft angle, and how far back you position the ball. Reducing the height of the trajectory may be advantageous because of wind or some overhanging obstruction such as tree branches.

This section gives some useful general advice that results from calculations with our computer model. We were able to show distance gain for moving the ball rearward in a single graph for the shorter irons. It is fairly good approximation for full swings for all golfer classes. Figure 3-2 gives this result. For short, we call this the *front-back factor*.

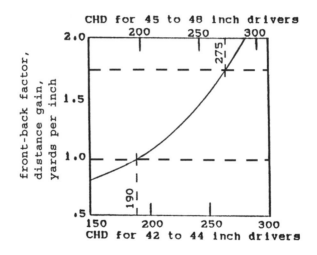

FIG. 3-2 *Estimating the distance gain for moving the ball back in your stance, the front-back factor. Moving the ball forward gives distance loss while moving it back gives distance gain. It applies only to full shots with irons shorter than the 6-iron. On the top and bottom scales, CHD means your center hit distance with long-shaft or normal drivers, respectively.*

To use Figure 3-2, first locate your CHD for your driver on the top or bottom scale as indicated in the figure. (CHD of your driver is an approximate indicator of your head speed and that is why we used it in Figure 3-2.) Notice that the top scale is for long club length drivers and the bottom scale is for medium and traditional club length.

There are two examples shown by dotted lines in the figure.

In the lower example, CHD is 190 yards. The dotted line goes up to the curve and then left to show that the front-back factor is a 1.0-yard gain of distance for each inch rearward. In the upper example, CHD is 275 and the dotted lines show that the front-back factor is about 1.7 yard per inch rearward. For playing the ball 5 inches rearward, this is 1.7 times 5 or 8.5 yards. In the first example, the front-back factor is 1.0, which is 5-yards gain for 5 inches rearward (1.0 times 5).

The 6-iron and longer clubs give progressively smaller front-back factors. For golfers who have reasonably long drives, the factors are about half as large for a 4-iron and about a tenth as large for a 2-iron. Corresponding factors for very long hitters are somewhat larger, and for short hitters, smaller.

If you move the ball forward, there is a loss in CHD instead of a gain. Of course, you can't move the ball forward more than an inch or 2 without danger of taking too much turf before the clubhead reaches the ball. With drivers, a taller tee avoids the problem and you can move the ball forward.

Playing the ball back is helpful in some cases such as deep grass because the clubhead travels a shorter distance through the grass before it hits the ball. Some golfers do this when the ball is partly in the water for the same reason: the clubhead travels through a shorter distance of water. So, stated otherwise, playing the ball back reduces the distance of clubhead travel through grass or water, and thus the corresponding loss of clubhead speed and distance of the shot.

Figure 3-2 is an approximation. It applies to balls that hit the green and stop on the green. If the balls land and stop on the fairway, it is a poorer approximation.

It is important to know that moving the ball back or forward in your stance also somewhat alters the direction of the shot. You must practice to learn the needed correction of direction.

All you need to know to make use of the information in the graph is to remember the number of yards per inch for your particular CHD with your driver, and that this applies only to full swings with irons shorter than the 6-iron. You need not refer to Figure 3-2 again.

Span—The Up-Down Range for the Club Face

Hitting too high or too low on the club face is a problem for many golfers, and for all golfers in difficult situations. This chapter will provide you with a better understanding of the up-down leeway—or span—on your club face for good ball contact with various clubs on various kinds of grass and on hardpan (the common term for bare or nearly bare soil or a pathway).

The message of this chapter is that the more lofted clubs should be avoided when hitting from thin grass or hardpan. You should have much less concern when the ball sits higher above the soil such as in good fairway grass. This is not news to most golfers, but many will find it to be worthwhile to know more about the details.

Golfers know that they will get very poor shots if they hit too high or too low on the club face. For the longer irons on good fairways, there is a satisfactory in-between range of about 3/4 inch. We call this up-down leeway for good shots, the ***span*** or ***H***.

In this chapter you will learn more about the span in more specific and useful terms than usual. This is mostly new information which has never been published and is based on our measurements. While you have about 3/4 inch span for the longer irons on good fairways, with the shorter irons and wedges, you may have less than half as much span. Very short grass (tight lies) and especially hardpan can reduce span to zero (no up-down leeway) or even make it negative for wedges. Span deserves serious attention. This discussion is concerned with clubs other than drivers and putters.

When you swing too low, the bottom of your club face strikes too far down into the turf (or soil). When you swing too high, you top the ball, meaning too much of the imprint of the ball impact occurs at the bottom of the club face. Span is our name for the vertical distance from the lowest position on the club face to the highest position for good shots. It is important to know how much span there is between too low and too high, and to understand what makes span larger or smaller. A good acquaintance with span will help you to minimize these problems.

The span depends strongly on how high the ball rests above the soil, and we call this distance the ball-ground distance, or **BG**. Table 4-1 shows what our measurements indicate about how BG varies with various kinds of grass.

TABLE 4-1 *Ball-ground distance BG for various kinds of grass.*

	GRASS (BG), inches
short rough, damp area (bluegrass)	.861
short rough, normal (bluegrass)	.552
fairway, normal (bluegrass)	.346
tee (bentgrass)	.140
grass at margin of putting green (bluegrass)	.08 to .32
putting green (bentgrass)	.040
hard pan and pathways	.000

As noted, the span depends on how deeply the sole of the clubhead is allowed to dig into the soil when making contact with the ball. We call this dig distance **DD**. We made various tests and found that DD is about .13 inch for normal fairways, .08 inch for tight lies, and 0 for hardpan. When the dig distance is greater, the shot is strongly affected.

Table 4-2 shows how the span varies for various golfer types for full hits on normal fairways, tight fairways, and hardpan such as pathways. It depends on the golfer type because the stronger

TABLE 4-2 Up-down span (H) in inches for good ball contact with full swings for golfers A, B, and C, for normal, tight, and hardpan lies. Normal lies use BG = .35 inch and DD = .13 inch. Hard lies use BG = 0 and DD = 0.

club	A golfer			B golfer			C golfer		
	normal	tight	hard	normal	tight	hard	normal	tight	hard
1W	.66	.43	.18	.68	.45	.20	.69	.40	.21
3W	.59	.36	.11	.62	.39	.14	.65	.42	.17
5W	.54	.31	.06	.57	.34	.09	.60	.37	.12
3I	.53	.30	.05	.56	.33	.08	.59	.36	.11
5I	.45	.22	-.03	.50	.27	.02	.53	.30	.05
7I	.38	.15	-.10	.43	.20	-.05	.46	.23	-.02
9I	.32	.09	-.16	.39	.16	-.09	.41	.18	-.07
PW	.30	.07	-.18	.37	.14	-.11	.38	.15	-.10
SW	.27	.04	-.21	.35	.12	-.13	.36	.13	-.12
W2	.25	.02	-.23	.33	.10	-.15	.34	.11	-.14

hitter (*golfer A*) will produce a larger ball imprint on the club face than either *golfer B*, an average hitter, or *golfer C*, a light hitter. This table is slightly altered and corrected from the *First Book*.

In Table 4-2, notice how the span diminishes rapidly when the turf tends toward tight and hard lies. These characteristics are important to keep in mind. This is a bit less critical for golfer C than for the harder hitters. The negative numbers show that with the more lofted clubs on hardpan, a near-normal imprint is not possible (too much is off the bottom of the face). You should avoid these clubs for very tight lies and hardpan.

To summarize, when the ball rests on the soil or very nearly so, it is best to avoid using the more lofted clubs, even if the shot you want is short. The reason is that the ball imprint is necessarily partly off the bottom edge of the club face and the shot can not be the same as for a normal lie. With a less lofted club and an easier swing, this problem is reduced or eliminated.

TABLE 4-3 *Up-down span (H) for short distances (partial swings) for a few clubs. The imprint diameter (ID in Figure 4-1) is much smaller than for full swings. The result is larger span. This figure applies to golfers A, B, and C.*

club	loft deg	distance yards	imprint diameter inches	H, inches	
				fairway	hardpan
3I	23	10	.16	.78	.36
9I	46	10	.17	.51	.05
W2	60	10	.18	.40	−.06
3I	23	20	.24	.80	.32
9I	46	20	.25	.48	.04
W2	60	20	.26	.38	−.08
3I	23	30	.30	.73	.29
9I	46	30	.31	.47	.04
W2	60	30	.32	.36	−.10

When you have a partial swing, the imprint diameter is much smaller, so the result is larger values for span. Table 4-3 is similar to Table 4-2 except it is for partial hits instead of full hits and shows this result for various clubs. Even though the imprints are small, the more lofted clubs still have negative values for span on hardpan where they should not be used.

If you get a good mental picture of these effects from the tables, you will be better able to judge when special care is needed and when the more lofted clubs should be avoided.

Hitting down on the ball by playing it back in the stance will increase span. This is because it lowers the effective loft angle. We studied such cases and concluded the result is nearly the same as addressing the ball normally with a less lofted club. Playing the ball back may be useful in deep grass or shallow water, but it doesn't help on hardpan.

If you want more detail on how and why these effects happen, you may wish to study Figures 4-1, 4-2, and 4-3. There is additional detail in the *First Book*.

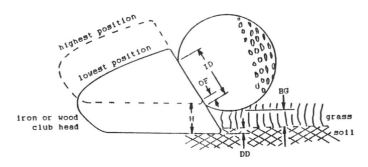

FIG. 4-1 *Illustration of span of up-down errors. H is the span. The grass holds the ball a distance BG above the soil. At the low extreme the club is allowed to dig into the soil a maximum amount defined by distance DD, and at the high extreme, 25% of the input area (shown at OF) is allowed to be off the bottom of the face.*

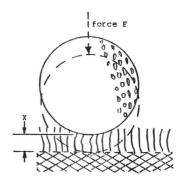

FIG. 4-2 *The ball is shown resting freely on the grass. A downward force F presses the ball farther into the grass as shown at X. We define ball-ground clearance BG as the value of X when F is 1.3 pounds. More force significantly deforms the soil.*

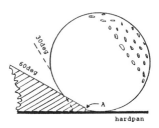

FIG. 4-3 *Illustration of the problem of using a wedge for shots from hardpan. You can see at A that the imprint is partly off the face with a 60 degree wedge, even with perfect contact. The dotted line shows that a less lofted club, such as 30 degrees, eliminates the problem and allows good shots even when the clubhead is somewhat above the hardpan.*

Effects of Wind on Shots

Wind often causes serious lateral and distance variations for your golf shots. This chapter will help you understand various ways to estimate the wind, its effect on various kinds of shots, and the corrections you can make to minimize the related errors in where your ball stops.

Golfer Skill Levels

We will consider golfers of various skill levels as in some other chapters. We arbitrarily define these skill levels as **golfer P** (professional), **golfer A** (excellent amateur), **golfer B** (average golfer), and **golfer C** (beginner or marginally skilled golfer). With formerly conventional drivers having 43-inch shaft length, 88-gram shaft weight, 43.5-gram grips, and 210-gram heads, these golfer levels have specific head speeds and handicaps. The respective head speeds for each of the four skill levels are 114.1, 100.7, 87.2, and 73.8. miles per hour. The respective handicaps for each of the skill levels are 0, 10, 20, and 27.5.

Effects of Wind on Golf Shots

Some of the main effects of wind are shown below in graphs and tables. A later section gives guidance for estimating wind in a way easily used by golfers. More detail is given in Chapters 14 and 15 in the *First Book*.

Figure 5-1 shows the general nature of the flight of a ball with and without wind. This is for ideal center hits by golfer B for 3 different clubs. To emphasize the effect of wind, we used an unusually large wind speed of 30 mph blowing toward the golfer at a 45 degree angle. Golfers rarely play in such winds. These calculations were for modern club designs with the driver's loft angle optimized for the B golfer. The particular design of the club is not important for this example of wind effects so long as the driver's loft angle is near optimum.

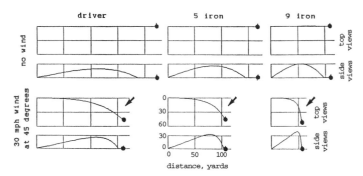

FIG. 5-1 *Samples of the effect of a strong wind on golf shots for golfer B. The upper graphs are for normal conditions with no wind and may be compared with the lower graphs having a 30 mph wind blowing toward the golfer, as shown by the arrows. The scale numbers on only one set of graphs along with the legend at the left and right apply to all graphs.*

In Figure 5-1, notice the legend at the right. It shows which are top views of the shot and which are side views (i.e., plan views and elevation views). The legend at the left identifies the graphs which measure the effects of the condition of no wind and the graphs which measure the effects of a wind of 30 mph. The top views with no wind are straight lines. With wind, the shots are strongly curved. The side views show that this wind condition increases the height and shortens the flight, bounce, and roll of the shots.

In this example, wind causes about the same loss of distance and about the same lateral error for all 3 clubs. Other head speeds give somewhat different results.

Figure 5-2 shows the computed scatter of ball stop-points of 500 shots for golfer B with a strong wind of 20 mph coming from any of the 4 directions indicated by the arrows. For each of the 500 shots, the computer randomly selected values from the statistical distributions of each of the 5 main golfer errors which will be discussed in Chapter 7. Each circle shows a single perfect center hit where the golfer has none of these usual errors. The small circles are center hits for golfer C, the intermediate ones are for golfer B, and the large ones are for golfer A. The scatter of ball

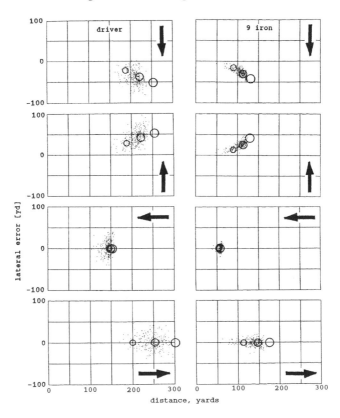

FIG. 5-2 *The effect of 20 mph wind on ball stop-points on the fairway for golfer B with a driver and 9-iron. Arrows show wind direction. The larger circles are center shots for golfer A, the medium circles are for golfer B, and small circles are golfer C. The golfer skill levels are defined in the text.*

stop-points for golfers A and C are not shown, but they would be similar except being smaller and larger and would be approximately centered on the large and small circles, respectively.

The 3 circles in Figure 5-2, with wind toward the golfer, happen to cluster together more than for the other wind directions. This somewhat surprised us. The head wind can reduce the distance for shots with high head speed so much that the ball may actually stop with the same or less distance than for shots with low head speed. This is because the high head speed causes much higher shots, giving longer flight times and thus more time for the wind to alter the shots.

To explore the head wind effect further, we calculated the data in Table 5-1 to show center hit distances **(CHD)** for a variety of cases. It shows that this effect varies greatly with head speed, wind speed, and the club being used. The golfer skill levels are defined above. Wind affects the ball stop-point of shots much more for long hitters than for short hitters.

These examples are for normal wind conditions with no nearby hills, trees, or buildings. The effects of these factors are discussed in a later section.

Estimating Wind Speed

Golfers know that they must make corrections when the wind is blowing. Adjustments needed can become rather large when the wind is strong. In this section, we discuss various methods you can use to estimate wind speed.

In 1805, the **Beaufort scale** of wind speed was devised for the British Royal Navy. It is still a useful classification of wind speed. It is especially useful for golfers because it gives results as miles per hour, without instruments, and it's easy to use. Golfers may wish to learn the Beaufort scale in conjunction with other ways to estimate wind which we will discuss.

Table 5-2 lists the Beaufort scale up through Beaufort number 6. Not much golf is played when the wind speed is higher. The range of most concern to golfers is Beaufort scale number 2 through number 5, from about 2 to 21 mph.

Table 5-1 *Effect of head and tail winds on center hit distance for the 3 golfer classes (A, B, and C) with various clubs. For cross winds, the distance to the side is given from a no-wind stop point. It is about the same for wind from either side. HS means head speed and CHD is center hit distance in yards. Each 1 wood has optimum loft angle (LA) for the no-wind condition; other clubs use typical values for LA. Results are similar to Figure 5-2 for the 20 mph columns.*

club	golfer	HS, mph	CHD, no wind	center hit distance, yards						lateral dist., yards		
				head wind, mph			tail wind, mph			cross wind, mph		
				10	20	30	10	20	30	10	20	30
1 wood	A	104.4	253.0	218.3	173.2	123.9	278.3	295.3	305.6	23.4	47.2	71.2
1 wood	B	90.4	218.9	192.3	155.8	108.6	237.1	248.6	255.1	18.4	36.9	55.6
1 wood	C	76.5	180.9	163.1	137.0	100.7	192.4	199.3	203.2	13.0	25.9	38.8
5 iron	A	87.3	199.2	163.7	123.2	82.5	229.8	255.8	277.7	22.5	45.4	69.4
5 iron	B	75.6	171.3	145.8	115.9	85.7	192.7	210.6	225.5	16.0	32.2	49.2
5 iron	C	64.0	139.4	122.8	102.8	79.1	153.1	164.4	173.6	10.3	20.8	31.8
9 iron	A	82.1	128.5	97.2	60.2	21.5	154.4	175.8	193.2	19.7	40.3	62.4
9 iron	B	71.2	112.2	89.4	61.7	33.4	130.7	145.6	157.5	14.3	29.0	44.8
9 iron	C	60.2	92.4	77.3	58.7	40.4	104.3	113.8	121.1	9.4	19.0	29.1

TABLE 5-2 *The Beaufort Scale for wind (numbers above 6 are omitted). By permission of Merriam-Webster's Collegiate Dictionary, Tenth Edition, ©1999 by Merriam-Webster, Incorporated.*

Beaufort number	name	miles per hour	description
0	calm	<1	Smoke rises vertically.
1	light	2	Direction shown by smoke, but most wind vanes don't move.
2	light	5	Wind felt on face. Leaves rustle. Wind vane moved by wind.
3	gentle	10	Leaves in constant motion. Flags partially extended.
4	moderate	15	Raises dust and loose paper. Small branches move.
5	fresh	21	Small trees sway. Crested waves form on inland waters.
6	strong	27	Large branches in motion. Hard to use umbrella.

The Beaufort scale is easy to use but has its drawbacks. It is a good guide for wind speed but doesn't show direction very well. Also, trees, wind vanes, inland water, and umbrellas are not always available to observe. The Beaufort speeds are particularly useful as a guide or reference for calibrating other ways of judging the wind speed.

Here are various ways to estimate wind speed and direction:

1. Use the Beaufort scale—advantages and disadvantages are described above.

2. Toss grass or leaves into the air. This is the most common way for golfers to estimate wind speed and direction. Golfers merely need to observe which direction the grass moves and how fast and how far it moves. It is hard to estimate a speed number on the result, but it is good for estimating direction. We suggest comparing these

observations with the Beaufort scale at every opportunity to improve accuracy of your judgment.

3. Observe the appearance of the flag on the flagstick. This is helpful, but a flag is not always visible and it is often too far away to see the direction.

4. Obtain a "feel" for the wind. This can be very useful, quick, and easy. It is more successful if the golfer watches trees and other indicators related to the Beaufort speeds and, after observing for many times, learns how various Beaufort speeds feel. It is easy to face directly into the wind to estimate direction.

5. Use some kind of simple wind indicator. You can use a ribbon or some yarn and hold it above your head. You observe how far it swings upward in the wind and observe its direction. It is necessary to calibrate this method, such as with the Beaufort scale, in the same way as (4) above.

We think that (2) and (4) are good methods because of simplicity. Method (5) could be good, though there is the inconvenience of always needing an extra item.

We suggest that you memorize Beaufort numbers 2, 3, 4, and 5 listed in Table 5-2 by frequent use in order to calibrate the method you prefer.

Effects of Obstructions When There Is Wind

Obstructions such as trees and buildings can shield the golfer from the wind and thus make it difficult to estimate the wind effects. Obstructions forward from the golfer are not common but have more effect on shots with headwind than those to the side or rear. Serious students of the game may wish to study Chapter 14 of the *First Book.*

The Beaufort scale is helpful when there are obstructions because it refers to trees, leaves, and branches which often are the actual obstruction, and for trees, it provides wind estimates up and out where your ball will fly. Trees are often tall enough to avoid most effects of other nearby obstructions.

Air Drag, Feel, and Sound of Clubs

This chapter briefly discusses air drag on club shafts and heads; and the feel, sound, and appearance of clubs.

Loss of Drive Distance Caused by Air Drag on Head and Shaft

The essence of this section is: *You needn't worry about air drag on a large head or on the shaft when you swing a large-head driver.* Air drag only slightly reduces the distance you get.

Large heads provide important benefits. Recently driver head volumes and corresponding face areas have increased from about 160 cubic centimeters and 3 square inches to 300 and even 400 cc with 5.5 square inches or more. Larger faces have the advantage of fewer **POF** hits (partly off the face hits). This advantage is greatly enhanced when optimum face outlines are used as will be discussed in Chapter 8. In addition, these large volumes are conducive to larger moments of inertia which reduce the penalty for off-center hits. This is an important factor to make the sweet spot larger (even more important is proper curvature of the face surface.)

Shafts are being promoted which have unusually large diameter for the lower quarter or third of the shaft. This is advantageous for minimizing small variations of head orientation when your head speed varies slightly as will be discussed in Chapter 7.

Large club faces and large shafts have air drag which tends to slow the head speed. It is important to know if this air drag causes significant loss of distance. This question is important only for *maximum distance clubs* (drivers and the first fairway wood). It is unimportant for irons because you can always use a club with less loft if you need more distance. You don't have this option with the maximum distance clubs.

We were able to model this problem and draw clear conclusions. Figures 6-1 and 6-2 show the results in graphical form as explained in their captions. Note that **CHD** means "center hit distance." Figure 6-1 demonstrates that air drag causes loss of no more than about .5 or .6 yard for even extremely large club faces. Figure 6-2 shows that even when the shaft tip diameter is as large as .5 inch, distance loss is only about .5 yard.

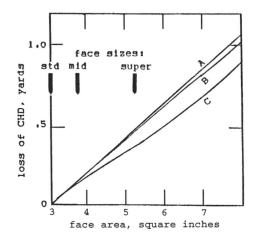

FIG. 6-1 *Loss of center hit distance (CHD) for large face drivers relative to CHD for a reference face area of 3 square inches. Shaft tip diameter is .335 inch. The curves are for golfers A, B, and C whose respective head speeds are 100.7, 87.2, and 73.8 mph.*

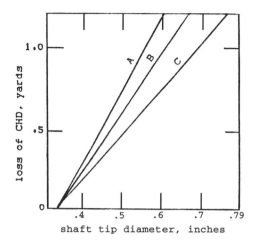

FIG. 6-2 *Loss of a driver's CHD for tip diameters which are large compared to that for a reference shaft diameter of .335 inch. Face area is 3 square inches. The curves are for golfers A, B, and C, whose respective head speeds are 100.7, 87.2, and 73.8 mph.*

The conclusion is that you needn't worry about air drag on the head or shaft. It is almost a negligible problem even for long hitters with high head speeds. This is true even for very large heads and very large shaft tip diameters. The *First Book* gives additional detail.

Feel, Sound, and Appearance

We believe that things such as feel, sound of impact, and appearance are only important on a transient basis and variations are not particularly important design factors. When a golfer becomes familiar with the use of a club and believes that it performs well, he or she will usually become accustomed to such things as feel, sound, and appearance and will come to consider these characteristics of the preferred club to be quite acceptable, even desirable. Accordingly, we consider them to have little long-term importance to club design. They may have promotional value for a manufacturer for a few years, but little or no lasting value.

We distinguish between "swing feel" and "impact feel." Swing feel seems to be mainly dependent on shaft flexibility and probably is unimportant except as a golfer's personal preference.

Remember that some golfers have learned to make good shots with trick or practice demonstration shafts that have a hinge part way down the shaft, and even with a short length of chain replacing a short length of shaft. Probably a favorable feel is simply the feel that is familiar to a golfer and is subject to large changes with practice and familiarity.

Golfer Errors for Full Hits

This chapter discusses errors and how they affect the design improvements discussed in this book. This is fundamental information that can help you to judge which parts of your game you may want to improve and can help with club purchase decisions. If you wish, you can skip this chapter without loss of continuity. Study of golfer errors is essential for optimum club design. Use of this data and our computer programs resulted in more forgiving and more accurate drivers and greater drive distance.

Errors and How They Combine

Finding and working with errors is, in some respects, the most important feature of our work. We classify errors as ***input errors*** and ***output errors***. Most input errors are caused by the golfer and we call them ***golfer errors***. Output errors are a measure of the scatter of stop-points of the shot. Input errors cause output errors.

The golfer's goal for every shot is to repeat the swing without variations so that at impact, there is always the same ***alignment*** of swing path (the "alignment"), the same clubhead orientation, the same head speed, the same location of hits on the club face, etc. Each golfer's variations from his/her own *averages* are what we call ***golfer errors***. In approximate order of decreasing effects on output errors, the principal golfer errors are variations of alignment, head speed, clubhead orientation, and the scatter of hits over the club face (we call this scatter the **hit pattern**.) For some purposes, other things may also be considered to be input errors, such as club designs which are far from optimum; and variations in the wind, weather, and turf. For drivers, we usually consider that there are club design errors if ideal center hits fail to reach the maximum distance that would be realized by an optimized design for the particular golfer's head speed.

By use of our computer model we can calculate output errors which are caused by any or all combinations of input errors. This allows us to evaluate the relative significance of the various input errors and—importantly—to find the optimum combination of club design features. For example, stop-point errors caused by a golfer's off-center hits can be compared with the stop-point errors caused by using a driver having loft angle (or other design parameters) different from what would be best suited for that particular golfer. Output errors are the basic way to compare the importance of various input errors and club design variations.

For all clubs, the model enables us to find the combination of features which minimizes the scatter of stop-points. In addition, for the **maximum distance clubs** (the driver and 1st fairway wood), the model allows us to find the optimum combination of club design features for best distance. The model avoids the nearly impossible problems of studying the effects of errors and design variations by direct experiments with golfers (these problems are caused by the interaction of factors which was discussed in Chapter 1.)

The model has another important advantage and that is finding effects which are very small and thus difficult or impossible to measure experimentally with golfers. This is also important because it shows which errors may be neglected so that attention can be directed to the most important effects.

It is the nature of the combination of most kinds of errors that the most important few sources of input error usually determine the resulting output errors (errors of stop-points). The numerous less important input errors contribute so little to the output error that they have negligible effects and can be ignored.

For example, suppose that you made numerous idealized shots for which you had only 2 errors. And suppose one was to randomly hit off-center toward the toe or heel and the other was random errors in orientation of the club head. If the off-center hits caused average scatter of stop-points of 5 yards and the average errors of orientation caused 5 yards, the combination of both errors is not the sum (5+5 = 10 yards), but more nearly, 7.1 yards. Furthermore, if you were able to reduce the orientation errors to 1 yard, the combination is not the sum (1+5 = 6 yards), but more nearly 5.1 yards. This illustrates that combined errors do not simply add together and—importantly—when the output error caused by one input error is much larger than that of another, it tends to mask or obscure the effect of the smaller error. A few errors *do* add in the simple manner which one might expect, but they are unusual in golf.

Accordingly, you should be aware that the output errors caused by only a few of your more important input errors usually obscure effects of all of the less important input errors to a far greater extent than most people would expect. This is important in golf club design. It applies widely to most kinds of devices and systems, including study of balls, golf clubs, automobiles, and even economic and political systems, though often extremely difficult to apply to such systems.

In golf, much promotional material emphasizes small improvements related to the less important input errors for which advantages are often real, but with imperceptible reduction in the output errors. Thus, their importance to the golfer is negligible. We believe this is an important fact to remember when judging claims of golf club improvement. The most important errors are shown in the figures of this chapter. These figures will help you to recognize which are usually the most important and unimportant features of club design.

If we assume you have a driver design which is well suited for you, your own errors (golfer errors) are most important. If your driver design is very poor, it is likely to magnify some of your golfer errors. This means that reducing your golfer errors by more practice may not improve the results as much as you hope. For example, if your driver's face surface is insufficiently curved, or is excessively curved, the driver can scatter your off-center hits excessively and hide or mask golfer errors in such things as alignment or clubhead orientation. Figure 7-4 is a good example and will be discussed later.

An important result of the combination of errors is that your first priority in practice and in selection of clubs is to work hardest to improve the 1 or 2 or 3 most important input errors and ignore the others, until you have conquered the worst or most important ones. While you may not always know which are the worst errors, we believe it is well worth your while to become acquainted with these details to help you to judge which items should concern you most.

Alignment, Head Speed, and Clubhead Orientation

We measured these golfer errors by means of strobe photos of golfers' swings, including golfers of various skill levels. From these photos we could make accurate measurements of the alignment, clubhead orientation, and clubhead speed just prior to impact. Next, for each golfer, we calculated the variations of these measurements from their mean values. These variations are the golfer errors in alignment, head speed, and clubhead orientation. In case you're interested, we express them as statistical "standard deviations."

Hit Patterns

Figure 7-1 illustrates the scatter of hits on a driver face for a high handicap golfer. The figure shows many imprints which are off, or partly off the face. These are shown as circular for illustrating their locations and are not actual imprints. We measured many such scatter patterns on numerous golfers. We used marking tapes on club faces to show location of impacts. We use the name "hit patterns" to describe the amount of this scatter (again as standard deviations of our measured hit patterns).

Excessive size of these hit patterns is an important golfer error. Hit patterns show the extent of off-center hits. When combined with a face outline, they show the frequency of **POF hits** which are hits partly off the face, a very important consideration for medium and higher handicap golfers. These POF hits appear less often with lower handicap because the whole hit pattern is more compact and far fewer are off the club face. Even tour pros are known to have POF hits on rare occasions. The frequency of POF hits is reduced by use of large club faces and especially so when the face outline shape approximates the shape of the hit patterns. POF hits are very detrimental and are more fully discussed in Chapter 8.

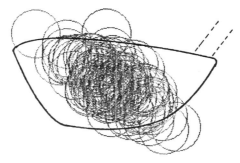

FIG 7-1 *The scatter of ball imprints on the face of a modern large face driver for a golfer whose handicap is 27.5. The imprint diameter is about half the ball diameter for this golfer.*

Output Errors

Our computer model, introduced in Chapter 1, allows detailed study of the stop-points of shots in the presence of various golfer errors. The examples discussed below will give you a good idea of which golfer errors cause which stop-point errors. For these examples, the inputs are the typical distribution of golfer errors in each case, based on our measurements with golfers and using the appropriate statistical methods.

Figure 7-2 shows how individual golfer errors (input errors) affect output errors for a representative case. The golfer errors are described or represented by the magnitude of variations, (the statistical "standard deviations"). For example, if you study the figure and the caption, you see for this case that the toe-heel scatter of hit points (dLA in the figure) are much more important than up-down scatter (dSA).

Figure 7-3 shows how these errors combine, starting with only one error in the upper graph and adding errors until all 5 are included in the lower graph. Note that the fourth and fifth input errors hardly increase the size of the scatter of stop-points. This illustrates that the input errors that have smaller output errors have little effect as was discussed at the beginning of this chapter.

Figure 7-4 shows how driver design improvement reduces the scatter caused by the hit pattern for 2 markedly different driver designs. The design improvements were mainly in enlarging the sweet spot and optimizing shape of the face surface curvature.

Figure 7-5 shows how the scatter of stop-points varies for the different golfer classes defined in the figure caption. Everything else being equal, longer distance always increases the scatter. This figure also shows the importance of lower handicap, with the result that the longer hits of golfer P have less scatter than the shorter hits of golfer C because golfer P has much smaller input errors than golfer C.

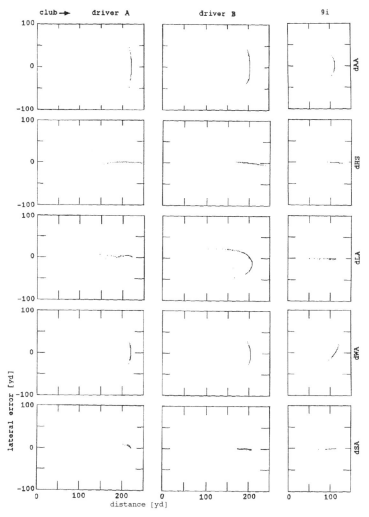

FIG. 7-2 *250 stop-points for each error when all other input errors are zero for golfer B, using various clubs. Driver A is our optimized large head driver design. Driver B is a laminated wood head from around 1980. At the right edge of the graphs, errors are identified, where dAA means alignment errors, dHS means head speed errors, dLA means the hit pattern errors in the long direction of the hit pattern, dWA generally means the open-closed angular errors of the club face at impact, and dSA means hit pattern errors in the short direction of the pattern.*

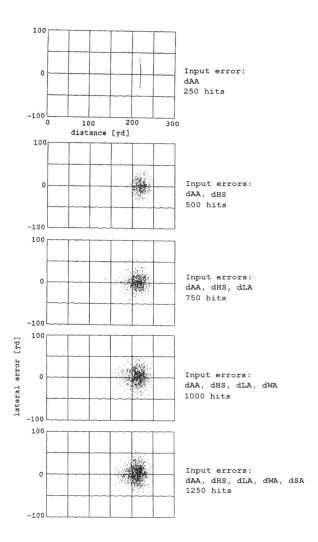

FIG. 7-3 *How individual golfer errors combine to cause scatter of the stop-points on a fairway for golfer B using driver A. See definitions in the caption of Figure 7-2.*

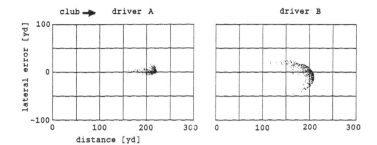

FIG. 7-4 *The effect of improved club design on scatter due to only dLA and dSA (hit pattern) for golfer B using improved driver A and driver B, an obsolete laminated wood design. See definitions in the caption of Figure 7-2.*

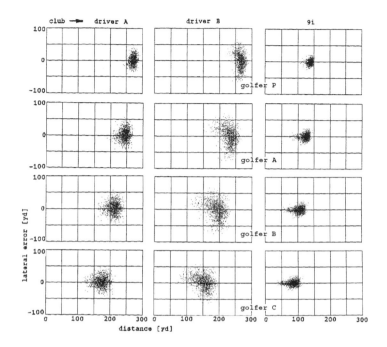

FIG. 7-5 *A general comparison of the scatter of stop-points for 4 levels of golfer skill. Each pattern represents 1250 hits. We arbitrarily define **golfers P, A, B, and C** as having respective head speeds for a standard 43 inch driver of 114.1, 100.7, 87.2, and 73.8 mph; and having respective handicaps of 0, 10, 20, and 27.5. Drivers A and B are defined in the caption of Figure 7-2.*

Optimized Designs That Suppress Errors and Gain Distance

This chapter describes how scatter of stop-points can be reduced and center hit distance can be increased for the maximum distance clubs. Optimum designs use a huge face with special surface and outline shapes. This face, with a large head, enlarges the sweet spot and reduces scatter, and minimize hits which are partly off the face. The best designs also optimize the combination of club length, shaft weight, head weight, center of gravity location, and loft angle to realize maximum center hit distance. This discussion will help you evaluate the great variety of promotional claims which are often made. Chapter 10 applies what is discussed here to help you to choose among drivers.

The Advantages of Large Clubheads

This chapter is concerned with the *maximum distance clubs*, namely the driver and first fairway woods, with emphasis on the driver. Large clubheads with large faces are very important to golfers, particularly for drivers. When the head and face are large, the moments of inertia of the head are large and this increases the size of the sweet spot. It is particularly important that large, properly shaped face outlines drastically reduce the likelihood of the occasional *POF hit* (a hit that is partly off the face—actually more than 25% of the normal imprint size is off the face).

In this chapter we will make frequent reference to *golfer classes P, A, B, and C.* They are defined in the Appendix.

THE HIT PATTERN. The subject of the hit pattern was introduced in Chapter 7. We measured the hit pattern by using hit tape (marking tape) on the club face. This tape leaves a visible imprint of the impact after each hit. We made these tests on numerous golfers. We measured the location of the center of each impact and studied the results statistically. Figure 8-1 shows a typical hit tape mark.

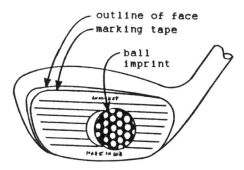

FIG. 8-1 *A typical marking tape imprint mark on a driver. We studied the diameters and locations of the centers of such imprints.*

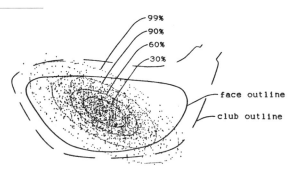

FIG. 8-2 *Typical distribution of hits on the face of a driver for a golfer of handicap 20, showing the elliptical distribution. Numbers on the ellipses indicate the percent of hits which will be inside of each ellipse. POF hits are indicated by the many dots near, or outside of, the edge of the face for this handicap.*

Figure 8-2 shows the general characteristics of the hit pattern on a driver for a golfer with **HCP** (handicap) 20. Each dot represents the center of a hit. As you would expect, the dots are grouped more densely near the center. This pattern was computer-generated, based on our measured statistical scatter of imprints. It closely represents real golfers.

In general the hits scatter in an elliptical shape (a football-like shape) which is tilted up at the toe end as shown. The upward tilt is greater for long-shaft clubs such as drivers, and less for the short irons. Hit patterns have a length about twice their height. Most hit patterns are about twice as long and twice as high for handicap 27.5 as compared with handicap 0. They are also somewhat larger as the club length increases, causing driver hit patterns to be a little larger than for a 9-iron. Putters have similar hit patterns, but smaller with little upward tilt at the toe end.

These hit patterns are for typical golfers. Individual golfers may have longer, shorter, wider, or narrower patterns than what is indicated for their HCP.

POF HITS AND LARGE FACE SIZE. Figure 8-2 shows that some hits are partly off the face. These are the hits which we call POF hits. They are common for high HCP and much less common for low HCP. Even the best golfers sometimes have them. These are probably the worst hits which golfers can make. The frequency of POF hits is much reduced for drivers when the face is large, and when the face outline shape is oriented to conform approximately to the hit pattern distribution. For most golfers, POF hits can be as important as the other 5 golfer errors that were previously discussed.

When the club design reduces POF hits substantially and improves accuracy, it is a significant factor for improving a golfer's confidence. Many golfers tend to ease back their swings to avoid POF hits. With optimized designs, the improved confidence encourages them to take stronger swings. The result is often markedly longer drives.

Figures 8-3, 8-4, and 8-5 show the scatter of typical imprints for various driver faces, as noted in the captions, for a 27.5 HCP golfer (golfer C). Some modern large face drivers (Figure 8-5) actually have slightly more POF hits than for Figure 8-4 because they are not quite as high toward the toe as the older style and not quite as low toward the heel. You can correctly conclude that large face area alone is not necessarily advantageous, unless it has an outline approximating the hit pattern shape.

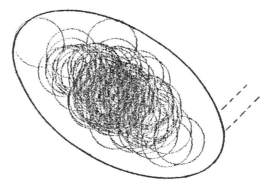

FIG. 8-3 *The scatter of imprints on an experimental 8.1 sq. inch elliptical face which is tilted upward at the toe for HCP 27.5. Here, 0.2% of hits are POF hits. These imprints were generated like those of Figure 8-2, except here, imprint outlines are shown and there, only the center points of imprints.*

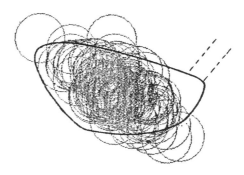

FIG. 8-4 *The scatter of imprints on a laminated wooden driver, representative of designs of about 1980 (driver B) for HCP 27.5. Here, 13.0% of hits are POF hits.*

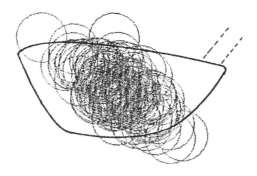

FIG. 8-5 *The scatter of imprints on a common type of large-head driver for HCP 27.5 (driver D). Here, 14.1% of hits are POF hits.*

Figure 8-3 illustrates the remarkable improvement possible for an extremely large, tilted, elliptical face, with only about .2% POF hits for HCP 27.5. A more practical design we have manufactured has a somewhat smaller elliptical face, tilted up not quite so much, with .9% POF hits for HCP 30. It is shown as driver A in Table 8-1 and is approximately comparable to the 27.5 HCP of Figure 8-3.

TABLE 8-1 *The percentage of POF hits for various drivers. Driver A is a driver which we designed, having a very large elliptical face with the toe tilted prominently upward and is slightly smaller than the driver of Figure 8-3. Driver B is a traditional wood clubhead, popular in about 1980. Driver D is a modern large head driver.*

handicap	driver A	driver B	driver D
0	0.0	0.6	0.8
10	0.0	7.8	8.3
20	0.2	10.2	11.4
30	0.9	13.9	15.0

Table 8-1 compares results for these club faces, illustrating the dramatic reduction of POF hits by use of an improved driver design. It shows that even a typical scratch golfer with a modern large head driver (driver D) gets .8% POF hits but essentially 0% for driver A. Golfers at all skill levels have less than 1/10th as many

POF hits when using driver A as compared with drivers B and D.

This work justifies the conclusion that an important reduction in POF hits results from tilting the toe more prominently upward and from using a larger, better face outline shape.

LARGE INERTIA AND LARGE HEADS. The importance of large moment of inertia for a clubhead has been much publicized, and justifiably so. **Moment of inertia** measures how difficult (large inertia) or easy (small inertia) it is for the clubhead to be turned during impact of hits that are off center.

The most important moment of inertia is measured about a nearly vertical axis through the *cg* (center of gravity) of the clubhead. Values about other axes are generally less important. The moment of inertia grows very rapidly as the clubhead size grows for a given clubhead weight.

A common and correct observation is that large size and corresponding large moments of inertia make the sweet spot larger. In combination with optimum face surface curvature, discussed below, the result is noticeably better accuracy of shots.

For these reasons, it is important to realize that large faces and heads are very beneficial, on two counts: fewer POF hits and more tolerance for off-center hits. Some advertising has appeared which irrationally suggests that large size is unimportant. We strongly disagree for the reasons given here. Recent trends agree with us on this point.

Optimum Face Surface Curvature

Here is a discussion of the first basic improvement of face surface shape of woods since the advantages of bulge and roll were discovered (about 1890 to 1910). It was found by applying our computer model to the problem.

Face *surface* shape should not be confused with face *outline* shape, that was discussed above. The proper amount of bulge and roll helps reduce scatter of stop-points due to off-center hits. The improved face surface shape has most of its curvature located high toward the toe and high toward the heel. It has much less curvature or even no curvature downward from the center.

Figure 8-6 is like a contour map for each face surface. It illustrates the basic difference of the optimum curved surface shape (driver A) from the conventional bulge and roll illustrated by the other 3 driver faces.

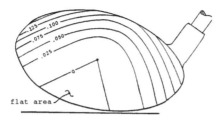

Driver A, our new scientific
face surface shape

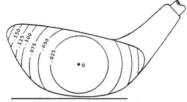

Driver B, a traditional wooden driver

FIG. 8-6 *The face surface shape for 4 drivers as shown by contour lines (similar to a contour map of terrain). The numbers on the curves are the distances in inches of the curved surface aft of a plane tangent to the face at the face center. The flat area for driver A is indicated. It is absent for other drivers.*

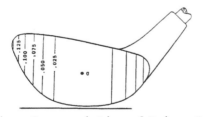

Driver C, a variation of Driver B

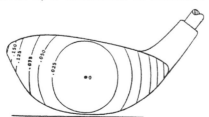

Driver D, a modern large face driver

These changes are not obvious by casual inspection. The special surface shape is easier to compare with another surface if one holds the edge of a ruler in various locations against each of the faces of clubs being compared, then looks at the gap between the ruler's edge and the club face. This makes it easy to notice the differences in curvature between club faces.

This improved face surface design causes substantial reduction of scatter of stop-points as was shown in Figure 7-4 of Chapter 7 even without considering POF hits. Golfers have found the benefits of the improved surface shape to be readily perceptible. A typical comment is "fewer shots off the fairway."

Similar improvements are possible for fairway woods, but for irons with the cg much farther forward, improvements are less and different in nature, and are essentially negligible for putters.

Optimum Combination of Head Weight, Club Length, and Shaft Weight

Testing to find the optimum club length and head weight combination for drivers is difficult and complicated because if one variable (factor) is changed, the best values of the other variables also change. For example if you want to judge if more or less head weight is best for you, probably you would simply try two drivers of different head weights. But it is not that simple, because the optimum club length and shaft weight or other parameters are different for each head weight. Furthermore, the 2 drivers being considered may or may not have loft angle best suited for you, and there are other differences. Finding the optimum combination of values for the various factors is another case where computers are invaluable.

We solved this problem with computer programs which were guided by a special test procedure used with numerous golfers (details are in the *First Book.*) We concluded that for drivers the practical optimum was a 46-inch club length with head weight of about 190 to 195 grams. Surprisingly, our tests show little variation of optimum club length or weight among men, women, golfer skill levels, strength, or size. Even lighter heads would gain a little more distance, but tend to be structurally too weak. This conclusion involved a small compromise to consider practical golfer and manufacturing requirements. Our conclusion agrees with modern trends toward greater club length.

For many years, driver club length was almost always 42 inches, head weight was about 210 grams, and the cg of the head was much too high. In recent years, the truth is emerging and driver designs use more appropriate values, with 10 or even 20 yards gain in center hit distance over those old designs. Additional gains of 3 or 4 yards over the better modern driver designs are not possible by any combination of shaft length, head weight, loft angle, or cg location. The "trampoline effect" is related and is briefly discussed in Chapter 10.

Designs for long distance champions are somewhat different, but the same methods apply.

The Optimum Loft Angle for Maximum Distance Clubs

Loft angle **(LA)** is important for the *Maximum distance clubs* (the driver and the first fairway wood), and most golfers have a clear feeling about the LA which is best for their own game. We have studied the optimum LA at length and some useful observations resulted. It is well known that a strong hitter needs a smaller LA, but the optimum LA also depends strongly on the location of the club head's center of gravity. Also, some golfers have their hands more forward or rearward at impact as compared with the average and this can cause the optimum LA to change by 2 or 3 degrees. Various other things affect it such as the shaft stiffness and whether the golf course being played is soft with somewhat longer grass than usual or dry and hard.

It is a good idea for best results to try drivers having various loft angles, and this is much more important for long hitters than for short hitters. For fairly soft fairways, our calculations indicate that golfers who hit about 150 yards lose only about a yard of distance with LA as much as 5 degrees above or below their optimum. Golfers who hit 250 yards or more should be concerned with being within 2 degrees of optimum to avoid loss of about a yard. Hard fairways make the acceptable tolerance on LA a little smaller. Most golfers will be surprised by these rather wide tolerances.

Head or tail winds have important effects on the optimum LA for a driver. Our calculations show that best LA is about 2 degrees lower for a 10 mph head wind and a little less than 2 degrees higher for a 10 mph tail wind. These 2-degree changes give only 2 or 3 yards better CHD than using your normal club. For 20 mph head winds, the appropriate LA is about 5 degrees lower and for tail wind, about 4 degrees higher, and may affect the distance by 10 or 20 yards.

There is much more detail on these subjects in the *First Book*.

Shafts

This chapter explains why the ideal driver shaft would be stiff and very light, for short as well as for long hitters. Irons are less concerned with shaft weight.

The Cause of Shaft Bending

It has been commonly thought that the whipping action of a shaft during the swing can improve the distance of a golf shot. Our tests and analyses and those of other recent researchers show that this is a very small effect and is usually negligible. What is commonly called "centrifugal force" pulls away from the grip with a force 50 to 100 pounds or more at impact. This force acts at the center of gravity of the head which is off to the side of the shaft's axis. That is what bends the shaft (this force wouldn't bend the shaft if it were in line with the shaft axis.) In turn, the shaft bending alters the orientation of the clubhead at impact. Photos of the club at impact show that for all clubs the shaft is bowed away from the golfer (that is, it is bent so as to bulge away from the golfer, causing the toe of the clubhead to move downward.) For woods, the **cg** (center of gravity) is well aft of the club face, so the shaft is also bowed away from the target, raising the loft angle **(LA)** and making it appear that the head is racing toward the ball more rapidly than the shaft. This is probably why a whipping action was assumed. Centrifugal force has essentially no effect on the head speed. The shaft *does* bend back at the start of the swing, but no significant forward bending follows other than that caused by the centrifugal force. Several other researchers have reached the same conclusion.

The amount of shaft bending varies a little with a golfer's unintended variations in head speed. Such shaft bending varies the head orientation at impact and slightly increases the scatter of stop-points. Stiffer shafts have less bending variation and therefore slightly decrease the scatter of stop-points. It is a small effect, but it makes a stiff shaft preferable to a flexible one. We also found that it is much more important to increase bending stiffness in the lower quarter of the shaft than in the upper part.

For woods and particularly the driver, bending also affects the optimum LA because the optimum LA must be chosen to allow for the shaft bending. This means that shaft stiffness is a significant factor in head design. Shaft bending effects are more important for a golfer who has high head speed, and much less so for one with a slow swing. Unfortunately, stiff shafts weigh more and the extra shaft weight reduces center hit distance, so a design compromise is necessary and tends strongly to favor light shaft weight for drivers. This is limited by shaft strength. If too light, the shaft breaks too easily.

As was noted earlier, with practice, good shots can be made with a training club having a hinge or a short length of chain partway up the shaft. This is a convincing demonstration that shaft stiffness is not as important as commonly believed.

Those who are seriously interested in how and why shafts bend may wish to study Figures 9-1, 9-2, 9-3, and also Chapter 20 of the *First Book*.

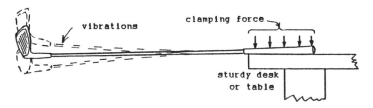

FIG. 9-1 *Vibrations of a golf club when its grip is held firmly against a rigid table or desk. To demonstrate this, hold the grip firmly against the table then ask a friend to pull up on the clubhead and quickly let go. It oscillates vigorously up and down.*

FIG. 9-2 *Vibrations of a golf club when a golfer holds its grip in the usual way. To demonstrate this, ask a friend to pull up on the clubhead and quickly let go, as shown. You will need to hold the grip quite firmly. The vibration dies out immediately and is very different from Figure 9-1.*

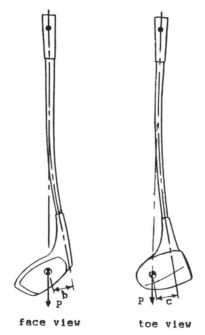

face view   toe view

FIG. 9-3 *The effect of centrifugal force, P, on the orientation of a driver head at the time of impact. The toe view shows that force P (which may be over 100 pounds), with moment arm C, bends the shaft and increases loft angle. The face view shows a similar effect in which the toe deflects down. Centrifugal force increases the loft angle and makes the face more open.*

Unsymmetrical Shaft Bending ("Spine")

Recently, much has been written about the supposedly important detrimental effects of shafts which bend more easily in one direction than another. This is often called the *"spine"* effect, presumably named after the spine of an animal. We studied this with experiment and theory and concluded that the spine effect causes negligible effects for the golfer. Details can be found in the *First Book*.

Shaft Weight

Shaft weight is of secondary concern for clubs other than the ***maximum distance clubs*** (driver and first fairway wood). The reason is that any loss of distance caused by more shaft weight is easily avoided by choosing a longer club, as noted earlier. Compared with graphite, steel shafts are heavier but have greater stiffness with correspondingly smaller variations of effective loft angle at impact due to variations of head speed. They also have a small advantage in higher torsional stiffness (that is, less "torque" in common, but technically erroneous, golf terminology). These are basic reasons why steel shafts tend to be a better choice for irons than graphite. Titanium and other materials have little or no advantage over steel shafts for the irons, however it appears that they can be about equally satisfactory.

Shafts are relatively important for the maximum distance clubs. Table 9-1 shows how increasing shaft weight reduces center hit distance, ***CHD***. In each case, with shaft or grip weight different from the reference line (top line in each of the 2 groups), head weight was maintained unchanged and optimum loft angle was calculated to best suit each new shaft and grip weight.

TABLE 9-1 *The effects of driver shaft weight and grip weight on center hit distance (CHD) for drivers for golfer P and golfer C, having respective head speeds for driver A of 114.1 and 73.8 mph. The top line in each group is a reference. Bold numbers are the changes of interest. The changes in CHD in the right column show significant gains for lighter shafts and little effect for grip weight.*

golfer type	shaft weight grams	grip weight grams	HS mph	CHD yards	change in CHD yards
P	*69.7*	*43.5*	*118.73*	*284.13*	*0*
P	**50**	43.5	119.86	285.90	+1.77
P	**90**	43.5	117.52	282.18	−1.95
P	**120**	43.5	115.55	278.90	−5.23
P	69.7	**30**	118.84	284.33	+.20
P	69.7	**70**	118.58	283.85	−.28
P	**0**	43.5	122.06	289.06	+4.93
P	**0**	**0**	122.19	289.29	+5.16
C	*69.7*	*43.5*	*75.81*	*184.41*	*0*
C	**50**	43.5	77.53	186.15	+1.74
C	**90**	43.5	76.01	182.41	−2.00
C	**120**	43.5	74.74	179.20	−5.21
C	69.7	**30**	76.86	184.55	+.14
C	69.7	**70**	76.70	184.09	−.32
C	**0**	43.5	78.95	189.37	+4.92
C	**0**	**0**	79.05	189.65	+5.24

There are 2 reasons for loss of center hit distance for heavy shafts. One is that a golfer can't swing a club with heavy shaft as fast as for a light shaft. The other is that most of the shaft weight does not affect the ball at impact. This is because the shaft bends during the short duration of impact and only a short length near the tip (a few inches) is rigid enough to participate in the head-ball impact. The extra effort to swing a club with heavy shaft mainly doesn't help gain distance for the shot.

It may be concluded from Table 9-1 that if manufacturers could reduce shaft weight by another 10 grams or so, only about 1 yard can be gained in CHD for drivers. Such reductions are difficult or impossible to achieve. Graphite shafts weigh less than steel, titanium, aluminum, or fiberglass shafts and are clearly the best choice for the maximum distance clubs (though they have little advantage for the irons and do tend to twist more.)

Another conclusion from Table 9-1 is that grip weight is relatively unimportant, the heaviest to the lightest causing a change in CHD of no more than about .5 yard.

Other Shaft Characteristics

Things such as vibration frequency or frequency matching and bulges high up in the shaft have little direct effect on those shaft stiffness and weight characteristics that have fundamental importance to a golf shot, *provided the designer has optimized the clubhead design for the head speed and the shaft being considered.* To be useful, the required shaft weight and stiffness characteristics must be known. Such characteristics as bulges and frequency which are indirectly related to stiffness do not define the essential details of the bending stiffness. High stiffness near the tip of the shaft is desirable and larger tip diameters promote this. Low bend points (or kick points or flex points) have no particular advantage and are somewhat detrimental because more shaft flexing close to the head causes greater change in effective loft angle at impact with a golfer's unintended variations of head speed.

Selecting a Driver

This chapter will help you to judge which driver is best suited for you. Chapter 8 explains the reasons behind the statements given here. Minimum scatter of stop-points and maximum distance are the usual goals for a golfer in choosing a driver and they are emphasized here.

Optimum Head Designs

HEAD SIZE. Chapter 8 explained why large heads for drivers substantially increase the size of the sweet spot and reduce scatter of stop-points. There are 2 design considerations which limit the maximum size of heads. One is structural weakness if the head is too large. The other is air drag on the head during the swing which reduces head speed. Air drag is nearly negligible with present large heads. The largest modern heads are near the limit of strength.

FACE OUTLINE AND SURFACE SHAPE. The occasional hit that is partly off the face is probably the worst hit in golf. A large face can nearly eliminate such hits, provided it is shaped approximately like the typical scatter of hits on the face, which we call the "hit pattern." Accordingly, while a large face is desirable, it is also important to be approximately elliptical in shape and markedly tilted up at the toe end in order to approximate the hit pattern.

The conventional surface shape of the face has bulge and roll (toe-heel curvature and up-down curvature). When the bulge and roll have the optimum curvatures (which is often not the case), scatter of stop-points due to off-center hits is materially reduced.

It is difficult to judge if bulge and roll are well chosen. Skilled golfers or golf robots can deliberately make toe and heel hits, and high and low hits on the face and judge the results after numerous trial hits. A driver having a large face and large moments of inertia helps reduce the scatter, even with poor face surface shape. Our new face surface is fundamentally different from the conventional bulge and roll shape, as was explained in Chapter 8. Together with large size, it has an optimum solution to the face surface problem. It gives perceptibly less scatter of stop-points.

To summarize, large face size, optimum shape of its outline, optimum shape of its surface, and large head size are all highly desirable.

GROOVES IN FACES. Grooves in faces of clubheads are less important than most golfers realize. In the late 1980s, the United States Golf Association had occasion to research the importance of grooves in much detail. It was found that grooves were unimportant except for the situation where short irons with high loft angles are used in conditions such as the short rough. Here, grass blades could be squashed between the ball and the club face to act as a lubricant, an effect that is partially suppressed by grooves.

Modern oversize driver heads tend to be so large that the walls are thin and sometimes the face fails during the large loads of impact of head and ball. Grooves significantly weaken the face with the result that they slightly reduce the maximum perimeter weighting which can be used. For this reason we believe that grooves should be omitted on the maximum distance clubs.

THE TRAMPOLINE EFFECT. Currently there is much attention to the so-called trampoline or "spring-like" effect in which the face is designed to be thin and springy to increase launch velocity and thereby gain significant distance. The distance gain is mainly for hits very near the face center.

This effect is controlled by the Rules of Golf of the United States Golf Association in such a way that drivers having more than a slight trampoline effect are not conforming for competitions which honor the Rules of Golf. That includes most competitive golf events in the U. S.

Whether or not the trampoline effect rule is technically justified, we believe that this and all other rules must be followed. If they are not, illegal balls, more than 14 clubs, rules relating to penalty shots, and in fact, all of the rules could logically also be ignored. The result would be an easy, different game, where all golfers get good scores, a game where skill matters little, a "game" without rules! A golfer's handicap is meaningless if based on golf rounds which ignore the rules. Nothing says rules must be logical or perfect (and they aren't), but without rules, there is no game.

Shaft Selection

With drivers and the first fairway wood (the *maximum distance clubs*), extra shaft weight reduces head speed and therefore, distance of the shot. For this reason light shafts are advantageous for drivers at all levels of golfer skill and strength. High shaft stiffness is also important but less so than low weight. A designer must compromise between weight and stiffness. The compromise favors light shafts for the maximum distance clubs. High stiffness is more important for long hitters than for short hitters. For good club designs, stiff shafts are not detrimental for short hitters and flexible shafts offer no real benefit to short hitters. This is at odds with conventional wisdom. High stiffness in the lower quarter or lower third of the shaft is more important than in the upper part.

As noted earlier, there is a convincing example of shaft design to support this conclusion. It is a training club having a shaft with a hinge partway up the shaft which means there is no shaft stiffness at the hinge. With practice, good shots can be made with this design by both short and long hitters.

For maximum distance clubs, good grade graphite shafts suit these requirements better than other materials which are presently available. For the other clubs, high stiffness is desirable, but shaft weight is not particularly important. The reason is that a golfer can choose a longer club when more distance is needed.

High torsional stiffness (which is called "low torque", a misnomer) is probably desirable but not critically so. For all golfers, high torsional stiffness is not detrimental.

Our research indicates that 46 inches is a good choice for driver club length for long and short hitters, whether male or female.

Grips

There has been some interest in light weight grips, especially for drivers. The effect of heavy grips is only a fraction of a yard loss of drive distance, depending little on golfer skill and strength, according to our presently available data. Our tentative conclusion is that if you happen to favor a large, heavy grip—and golfers with arthritis problems often do—don't be concerned about its weight. Conversely, ultra light grips are only very slightly helpful. We hope to examine this question further, time permitting.

Tests You Can Make

Use 2 or more driver designs each of which gives good center hit distance. It is probably better for comparison to hit alternate shots with each driver. You may be satisfied by a conclusion from tests on a driving range. It is best to play several rounds of golf with each, perhaps alternating drivers from one hole to another. Keep track of the distance and of the number of your hits which are off the fairway. Also keep track of hits which you think were partly off the face. On a driving range you can deliberately make off-center hits, 1 or 1.5 inches toward toe and heel and compare results.

Even a casual comparison takes much time and effort, unless a marked difference becomes immediately apparent. It is important not to compare the drivers being tested when one is used in conditions different from the other. Comparisons are not valid when there are changes in wind, turf conditions, how you feel, etc. A particularly difficult aspect is that it often requires much time and familiarization for a golfer to get the most out of a driver and to become accustomed to its performance, appearance, sound, and feel.

Summary of Driver Selection

The best choice for all golfer skill levels for the maximum distance clubs is a club length of about 46 inches with a light, stiff graphite shaft. Larger than usual shaft tip diameter is desirable. The head weight should be light, about 190 grams. There are important advantages for large heads, and for the driver, the face size should be large. The face outline shape is best if large, if at least somewhat elliptical in shape, and is prominently tilted upward at the toe and downward at the heel. The face surface curvature should be optimized for minimum scatter of stop-points, and this is harder to judge (see Chapter 8). Grip weight is relatively unimportant.

Putters and Putting

Our model for analyzing golf club performance also applies to putters and putting. In this part of the game, golfer errors and other input errors are rather different from the rest of the game. In this chapter, you will find some new data on the aim distance. You will also find some basic data on scuffing too deeply into the grass; the flight, slide, and roll of putts; and a discussion of unnecessary putting errors and misconceptions. Finally, there is a discussion of the comparison among putter designs, concluding that there is little difference in performance among them. The *First Book* gives much more detail.

Introduction

With minor modifications, our model is useful for analysis of putter design and performance in the same ways as described above for the other clubs. It has the same advantages of coping with many factors (variables) which greatly complicate field testing. Here, we will summarize only the general results. The *First Book* provides the detail for those who are interested.

Aiming Putters and the Aim Distance

Aiming. Two particularly important factors in aiming putters are: (1) keeping the face square to the intended launch direction and (2) proper ***alignment*** of your swing which means to make sure the swing path at impact is aligned with the launch direction. Of course properly reading the green (estimating the launch direction and speed) is probably the most important thing of all.

Keeping the face square requires careful observation of the face. Figure 11-1 illustrates the importance of correct face orientation. On a 10-foot putt, as an example when there are no other errors, an error of only 2 degrees as pictured, causes a lateral error of 4.2 inches at the hole. This lateral error is proportional to the distance. For example, it is 2.1 inches for a 5 foot putt and 8.4 inches for a 20 foot putt. As the figure shows, a 2-degree error is not easy to notice. *Good putting requires very close attention to proper orientation of the face.* Note that the face of the putter at impact should be squared to the intended ball launch direction (which is different from the target direction if the putt is expected to break.)

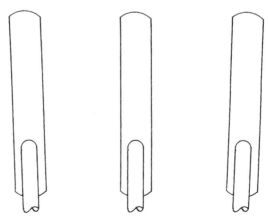

FIG. 11-1 *Compared with the center putter, the left putter is 2 degrees closed and the right one is 2 degrees open. These changes are hard to see, but cause large errors, for example, lateral error of 4.2 inches for a 10-foot putt.*

Much has been written about finding the proper swing alignment. One good idea for alignment is to lay 2 clubs 6 or 8 inches apart so that they are aligned with the intended direction of the putt. Learn to swing so that your putter head moves precisely through the path defined by the clubs.

AIM DISTANCE. The *aim distance* is our term for the distance *past* the center of the hole at which a golfer should aim for best results. Golfers are aware that it is important to plan their putts to stop somewhat beyond the hole ("never up, never in"). We researched this subject at length. We were able to calculate just how far past the hole one should aim to minimize the number of strokes to hole out. There are a few recent careful technical publications which reach some of the same general conclusions, but in different form, without the same degree of detail, and based on less direct testing on greens.

For practical use by golfers, the aim distance can be summarized in compact form as follows. You need only memorize the part which applies for your handicap and the "necessary adjustments."

- *0 handicap golfers should use aim distance of 7 inches for 5-foot putts, increasing to 13 inches for 20-foot putts, and diminishing to 7 inches for 40-foot putts.*

- *15 handicap golfers should use aim distance of 9 inches for 5-foot putts, increasing to 13 inches for 15-foot putts, and diminishing to 3 inches for 40-foot putts.*

- *30 handicap golfers should use aim distance of 12 inches for 5-foot putts, increasing to 14 inches for 10-foot putts, and diminishing to –3 inches for 40-foot putts.*

- *Necessary adjustments for all handicaps: For putts longer than 5 feet, add about 2 inches for very fast greens and deduct about 2 inches for very slow greens. For putts shorter than 5 feet, diminish the stated distances for 5-foot putts in proportion to the distance. For greens that slope significantly at the hole, the aim distance may be much less or much greater and experience is your best guide.*

These results agree with golfer experience and are a refinement on published aim distances. They apply to flat, level greens. Typical advice is 14 to 18 inches past the hole. In fact, the best aim distance is not constant, but rather, varies as stated above.

The *First Book* shows how aim distance depends on putt distance, green speed, and handicap, as approximated by the preceding paragraphs.

EFFECTIVE HOLE DIAMETER. It may help you to know that the effective hole diameter is significantly larger than its actual diameter of 4.25 inches, especially for slow greens. A ball which stops just outside of the edge of the hole will drop if the grass is tall enough. That is because the blades of grass away from the hole push the ball toward the hole and there are no corresponding blades of grass inside of the hole to push back. Table 11-1 shows the result of our experiments on this effect. For low **Stimp** (green "speed") such as 6 feet, the hole effectively grows .64 inch larger in diameter, whereas for Stimp 9, it is .43 inch larger.

TABLE 11-1 *Effective hole diameter is larger for slow greens.*

Stimp feet	diameter inches	increase inches
∞	4.25	.0
15	4.51	.26
12	4.57	.32
9	4.68	.43
6	4.89	.64

Scuffing the Grass When Putting

We studied the problem of scuffing the grass with the putter sole while putting. For most golfers, it is reasonably common to have slight scuffs which are not noticed and have negligible effects. A golfer rarely feels even rather deep scuffs, though they can cause significant loss of putt distance. When a scuff is strong enough to *feel*, the putt distance is drastically reduced, such as by 50%. The opposite of a scuff error is to top the ball, something that happens rarely. Our research suggests most golfers have the putter head somewhat too low at impact. They risk an occasional, unnoticed scuff and unexpected loss of intended putt distance. The *First Book* gives more detail.

To minimize scuffs, we designed a putter with a rail under the head to reduce the drag when there is a scuff. Even so, scuffs probably deserve more attention. We have found no serious discussions of scuffing in the past.

You might want to experiment with putts. Swing lower numerous times until you often notice a few scuffs. Then try numerous putts to see how high you can swing before you notice a few cases where you top the ball. Of course, serious topping of the ball causes a different feeling of the hit and drives the ball somewhat downward into the soil with attendant loss of putt distance. Your ideal swing would then be about halfway between. Marking tape on the putter face can be helpful in such experiments.

Impact, Flight, Slide, and Roll of a Putt

On every putt with a typical putter, the ball is launched slightly upward with a little back spin. It flies a short distance, then after negligible bounce, it slides in the grass and begins to pick up rolling action, until it rolls without sliding for the remainder of the distance. There are situations where you may want to know how far your putt flies, slides, and rolls. The model calculates the very short flight distance. We made experiments of the sliding friction of the ball on grass to study the sliding phase. We also made experiments about how the speed of the green affects the roll distance after sliding stops.

Briefly the result with typical putters with 3 degrees loft, for 5-foot to 30-foot putts, is that flight is about 5% of the total distance, sliding is about 10%, and pure roll is 85%. For very short putts, the pure roll part becomes nearly 100% of the distance. Pure roll is somewhat less than 85% for putts longer than 30 feet. Low Stimp greens have somewhat greater flight and slide distances. Putters with high loft have relatively slightly more flight and with low loft, have less flight.

An example of the use of this information might be putting from off the edge of the green. Suppose you have a 20-foot putt. The ball will fly about 5% of this distance or 1 foot, so if you're only a foot off the edge, the taller grass has little effect because the ball flight is mostly above the grass and the ball not sliding or rolling—it is the same as if the entire putt is on the green. This tells you that for shorter putts or when farther off the green, the taller grass must be reckoned with.

Irregularities of the Putting Green

We evaluated errors on level greens which are caused by irregularities of the green when no other errors were present. We found that on good greens, (in statistical terms) both distance and lateral errors caused solely by the green had standard deviations of about 2% of the putt distance. This means that for a 10-foot putt, if there are no other errors, 39% of putts would stop inside a 4.8-inch diameter circle, the remainder stopping outside the circle.

This deserves more research, but we expect that slower greens are worse and greens in poor condition must also be worse. The test putting machine is quite special and is used in a special way to preclude errors other than those of the green itself. For example, one must not repeat putts from the very same starting point, because the first putt leaves a slight, invisible groove in the grass which nearly eliminates lateral deviations and allows the 2nd putt to travel significantly farther. The machine demonstrated this very clearly. It must provide for exactly the same putt except for the position change, after it is moved to a nearby point on a new path. Dr. Clyne Soley wrote an interesting book, *How Well Should You Putt*, (©1977, Clyne Solely), in which he used a machine to make much the same experiment of putting without golfer errors. Unfortunately, his machine putts were not on a new line for each putt. His result was 88% success from 10 feet, roughly consistent with our observation of the need for using a new path for every test putt. Furthermore our result indicates that at 10 feet, his data on tour professionals show that they are nearly as good as a putting machine.

Where the Slope is Most Important

Many golfers believe lateral slope near the hole is far more important than elsewhere along the line of the putt. At the hole, the ball is moving slowly and has time to change direction much more than when it is far from the hole and moving faster. However, far from the hole, where slope causes only a small change in direction, the small change in direction acts over a large distance.

Analysis shows that lateral movement of the ball caused by slope is 50 to 60% greater when the slope is within a foot or 2 of the hole as compared with when the same amount of slope is near the golfer. This result depends little on Stimp or putt distance.

Thus, you must allow for side slope of the green near the ball and all along the path, even though slope near the hole is somewhat more important.

Unnecessary Putting Errors

Some golfers believe certain special techniques improve putting success. In fact, some of these are harmful to putting success.

PLUMB-BOBBING. Plumb-bobbing is commonly done. The usual process is to hold the putter by the top of the grip and let it hang down freely. According to one published description, the golfer stands behind the ball and aligns the shaft with the ball (or with the hole). In the golfer's view, the amount by which the hole (or the ball) appears on one side or the other of the club shaft is assumed to indicate which way the putt will break.

Plumb-bobbing is useless for directly judging the break of a putt in this manner. For a convincing example, consider a strong lateral slope between the ball and the hole, but with the hole and ball on spots of level ground. Plumb-bobbing would indicate that there is no break, when there actually could be a huge break.

On the other hand, plumb-bobbing may be useful for judging whether a spot on the green slopes left or right from your view. For that use, a level part of the green appears perpendicular to the shaft of a putter which is hanging freely.

To correctly judge the slope of an area of the green by plumb-bobbing, you must check to see if your putter shaft really does hang vertically. To do so, hold your putter by the top of the grip and check against the vertical corner of a building to see if the shaft matches the corner. If it does not, rotate the club around the shaft axis until you find the orientation where it really does hang vertically in your view. There are 2 orientations which do this, except for a very few designs where it doesn't matter. Either of these is the shaft orientation to use. Other orientations of the club give erroneous indications.

TOE PUTTS. Many golfers believe that on downhill putts, it is helpful to hit far out on the toe of the putter to give the ball a lower velocity when it leaves the putter. A slower swing accomplishes the same effect.

If you hit the ball slightly off center, it matters little if it is a *small* distance to one side or the other of the ideal place to hit (the sweet spot). This is not true when the hit is a *large* distance from the sweet spot. That is, for hits far out to the toe or heel, a small error in hit location makes a much larger distance error than a corresponding small error near the sweet spot. Hitting far out to the toe or heel also creates a small lateral error which must be accurately judged and compensated for in aiming.

Toe putting does not reduce the need to have the right head speed. It also requires that you learn how fast to swing for a situation different from your normal putting. Even worse, it causes significantly greater distance errors if you don't hit exactly where you intended on the face, as compared with similar errors of hitting near the sweet spot. From these considerations, we conclude that toe putting introduces unnecessary errors and cannot be as accurate as your normal putting.

CUTTING THE BALL. "Cutting the ball" in putting usually refers to a golfer making the head travel, not in the target direction, but strongly to one side, usually to the left for right-hand golfers while holding the club face square to the target or nearly so. The result is that the ball travels approximately in the direction in which the face is aimed and the ball starts with much side spin.

Some believe that the side spin somehow helps the ball drop into the hole on short putts. The fact is that side spin is quickly eliminated by sliding friction on the grass in the early part of its travel.

It is easy to demonstrate that side spin is quickly eliminated by making such a putt on a *level* green. You can observe that the ball travels a straight line (very close to the starting point you may be able to see a slight curvature for long putts.) Calculations show only a very slight curvature in the first few percent of the travel and none at all for the rest of the distance. There is none of the aerodynamic curvature (hook or slice) which accompanies a long flight from a long club when the ball has side spin.

Trying to cut the ball is another example of a golf stroke having unnecessary additional inputs which add to the errors inherent in the simplest stroke. Additional error sources are the new direction of travel of the head, the amount by which the club face is open, and the needed change in head speed.

Golfers who cut the ball usually succeed because they use it only for very short putts. Cutting the ball reduces the probability of success of a putt.

GRAIN OF THE GRASS. Blades of grass tend to lean to one side or another, depending on various things. Possibilities are the direction of the mowing, the slope of the green, and perhaps the direction of the sun when the grass is growing fastest.

Tests on a good bentgrass green with our precision putting machine showed no apparent effect due to grain of the grass. Bermuda grass may behave differently. This could be studied more carefully at various directions on an especially level green. If a golfer corrects for grain and its effect is negligible, another unnecessary additional error is introduced.

A special kind of putting machine is needed to make this study. It was discussed in the above section "Irregularities of the Putting Green" and in the *First Book*.

EYES OVER THE BALL, KEEPING THE PUTTER SQUARE. Most golfers know they should have their eyes over the ball at address. When your eyes are not over the ball, there is a change of the apparent ideal direction of the swing. Practice can make that OK, only if you can closely repeat this eye position. It is easier to repeat the "eyes over the ball" position than some other, less-well defined location.

Various putter features are advertised which claim to assure that your eye is vertically above the putter head, but they do not serve this purpose. Typically there is a line or mark low on the putter head and a related feature higher on the putter head. You are expected to adjust your eye position until the upper feature is centered over the lower, from your view point. This only assures that you are looking squarely toward the putter head, not that your eye is vertically above the head. To convince yourself, hold such a putter far out from your toes or even hold it out horizontally at eye level. You'll be able to tilt the toe up or down and find a position that aligns the 2 aiming features, even though you are very far from looking straight down with your eyes over the ball.

In general, golfers should avoid rotating the putter head during the back swing and the downswing, as is widely recognized. This is because if the head rotates, you must bring it back to the intended orientation at impact. Additional errors creep in if you are unable to bring it back as intended. Keeping it square minimizes this problem.

GENERAL CONCLUSION. For any putting stroke (or for that matter, any golf stroke), unless there are important advantages, there is no logical reason to do things which are not essential, if any of the other things you might do could possibly add errors to your basic golfer errors. In other words, *"keep it simple."*

A Comparison of Putter Designs

We did extensive computer simulations that calculated the number of putts to hole out as affected by putter designs. It was surprising that the differences among various modern putter designs are essentially negligible. On average, the analysis showed that dozens or even hundreds of rounds would be played before even one stroke would be saved by the best design. In actual play, only extensive tests done with extreme care could show this minimal difference. An important result is the conclusion that a golfer should stay with the putter he likes best, purely for reasons of self confidence. A feeling of satisfaction with a putter is important and is probably the strongest consideration in putter choice. The confidence aspect is one of the severe difficulties in using golfer putting results to compare various putters, as with many other kinds of testing in golf.

Chapter 36 in the *First Book* gives more detail on comparison of putters, and Part 4 gives support for the above discussions. The method of calculating putts to hole out deserves special attention from those who are technically oriented.

Appendix

Definitions of Key Terms

aim distance is the distance past the hole to aim putts on level greens for best results.

alignment or alignment angle is the angle between the path of the clubhead at impact and the target direction.

B&R means "bounce and roll" distance (sometimes called ZBR).

BG is the distance from the bottom of the ball to the ground. It varies with the nature of the turf.

cg means center of gravity and usually refers to the clubhead.

CHD (center hit distance), the flight plus bounce and roll distance for an ideal center hit.

dAA means standard deviation of variations of alignment.

dHS means standard deviation of variations of head speed.

dLA means standard deviation of variations of hit pattern in the long direction of the hit pattern.

dSA means standard deviation of variations of hit pattern in the short direction of the hit pattern.

dWA means standard deviation of variations of the open-closed angular errors of the club face at impact.

DD is the maximum distance by which the clubhead is allowed to dig into the soil at impact for a good hit.

Driver A is our optimized large head driver design.

Driver B is a laminated wood head popular around 1980 with center of gravity much too high.

FF aiming is a new way to aim, so-called because you look at the face in 2 separate steps (Chapter 2).

first fairway wood is the wood used on the fairway which is preferred when maximum distance is desired.

front-back factor is a factor used for estimating your distance gain for moving the ball back in your stance (Chapter 3).

golfers P, A, B, and C. With formerly conventional drivers having 88-gram shaft weight, 43-inch shaft length, 43.5-gram grips, and 210-gram heads, these golfer levels have specific head speeds and handicaps. The respective head speeds are 114.1, 100.7, 87.2, and 73.8 miles per hour; and respective handicaps are 0, 10, 20, and 27.5. The skill levels correspond roughly to professionals; excellent amateurs; average golfers; and beginners or infrequent golfers and many lady golfers.

golfer errors are the input errors which are caused by the golfer (Chapter 7).

H (see span)

hit pattern is the scatter of hits over the club face.

input errors cause output errors and include the golfer errors, and for some purposes, other errors.

maximum distance clubs are the driver and 1st fairway wood.

output errors are a measure of the scatter of stop-points of the shot.

POF hits means hits which are hits partly off the face (Chapter 8).

regrip means to change the club face orientation and take a new grip without changing orientation of your hands (Chapter 2).

span, also called H is our name for the distance from the lowest position of the clubhead to the highest position or good shots (Chapter 4).

Stimp reading or Stimp is the widely-used method of measuring if the green is fast or slow (the green speed).

turntable means to change the club face orientation by using the turntable movement in which you move your feet to reposition yourself as if on a turntable centered on the ball (Chapter 2).

working the ball is a term commonly used to mean making controlled slices or hooks.

Reference

The *First Book*
Frank D. Werner and Richard C. Greig, *How Golf Clubs Really Work and How to Optimize Their Designs* ©2000, 187 pages, 37 chapters, 76 figures, 28 tables, index.

This reference adds technical back-up information which supports and explains statements above. It reports 10 years of intensive research by the authors. Both are aerospace engineers with advanced degrees. Causes and effects are made clear in nearly all cases. The general text is readable most serious golfers. The technical parts are separated into Technical Notes.

Index

Refer also to the Appendix for definitions not listed below.

About the Authors

FRANK D. WERNER received his B.S. degree in physics at Kansas State University and his M.S and Ph.D. degrees in aerospace engineering at the University of Minnesota. He was the founder of Rosemount Engineering Company (now Fisher-Rosemount, a division of Emerson Electric Company). This company developed and manufactured precision instrumentation widely used in the aerospace industry and in America's space program. He later founded Origin Inc, a small R&D firm. Origin Inc developed the Novus windshield repair system which was the first successful repair method and continues to be the world leader. At Origin, he and Richard C. (Dick) Greig conducted fundamental research on golf for over 10 years, resulting in the BIGFACE 1 driver and the SCUFF-RAIL putter, then formed Tech Line Corp to commercialize these products. He has over 80 patents. Werner and his wife, Alice, live in Teton Village, Wyoming.

RICHARD C. (DICK) GREIG has earned B.S. and M.S. degrees in aerospace engineering from the University of Minnesota and has completed all course work for the Ph.D. degree in aerospace engineering from the University of Minnesota. He is adept at computer modeling of physical processes, the most notable golfing application to date being Tech Line's drivers and putters. He is currently president of Tech Line Corp. He is co-inventor with Werner on numerous patents. Greig and his wife, Judy, live in Jackson, Wyoming.

The **BIGFACE 1** Driver

Here are photographs of the large face driver (BIGFACE 1) which we designed using the methods described in the book and which is referenced in several places. Many consider it to be strange looking, even ugly and some object to the loud sound of impact. Users consistently report that it gives perceptibly better accuracy ("fewer shots off the fairway"; it is "easier to hit"; it "improves confidence in the game"; and some even say "took 10 strokes off their handicap".) They learn to like its appearance and to disregard its sound. It was designed according to the methods outlined in this book for top performance, without regard for appearance and sound. It conforms to the USGA Rules of Golf.

U.S. Patents 5,366,223, 5,380,010; others pending   © 2001 TECH LINE CORP

A Unique Book!

Most parts of this book are very useful and easy reading for any golfer, such as:

- *Aiming putters*
- *Aiming other clubs: slice control*
- *When the ball position is moved back*
- *Wind effects*
- *Air drag on club heads*
- *Up-down range for the club head*
- *Golfer errors*
- *The sweet spot*
- *Chapter 37 summarizes these and other useful topics*

Some parts are more complex and of interest mainly to more serious golfers and researchers. The book reports on experimental and theoretical research carried out over the last 10 years by 2 aerospace engineers in a full-time, dedicated research effort.

RETAIL ORDER FORM *Fax, Phone or Mail*

Visit our website at www.techlinegolf.com

By Fax: *Copy or remove this form, fill out, enter your Visa or MC card number, and sign. Fax to **307 739-1530**.*

By Phone: *Have your Visa or MC card number ready and phone **800 451-8858**.*

By Mail: *Fill out form, enter your Visa or MC card number and sign or include personal check (U.S. dollars only), add 6% sales tax for Wyoming residents, and mail in envelope to Tech Line Corp, 3975 S Hwy 89, Jackson, WY 83001.*

TECH LINE CORP

☐ Please send _____ copies of ***Better Golf from New Research*** for $18.95 (includes $4.00 S/H).

☐ Please send _____ copies of ***How Golf Clubs Really Work and How to Optimize Their Design*** *(First Book)* for $34.95 (includes $5.00 S/H).

☐ Please send descriptive brochure on **BIGFACE 1** drivers.

☐ Please send descriptive brochure on **SCUFF-RAIL** putters.

Name ....

Address .... Email (optional) .... Phone ....

City .... State .... Zip ....

Payment: ☐ Visa ☐ MasterCard ☐ Check   Card Number .... Exp. Date ....

Print Name .... Signature ....

DATE DUE